Signs of Hope and Health in Mainline Churches

ALSO BY THOMAS G. KIRKPATRICK

*Small Groups in the Church:
A Handbook for Creating Community*

*Communication in the Church:
A Handbook for Healthier Relationships*

*Better Ways to Better Relationships in the Church:
Guidelines for Practicing Humility, Experiencing Empathy,
Feeling Compassion, Showing Kindness, Expressing
Appreciation, and Doing Justice*

Signs of Hope and Health in Mainline Churches

Guidelines for Creating Hopeful and Healthy Congregations

THOMAS G. KIRKPATRICK

WIPF & STOCK · Eugene, Oregon

SIGNS OF HOPE AND HEALTH IN MAINLINE CHURCHES
Guidelines for Creating Hopeful and Healthy Congregations

Copyright © 2025 Thomas G. Kirkpatrick. All rights reserved. Except for brief quotations in critical publications or reviews, no part of this book may be reproduced in any manner without prior written permission from the publisher. Write: Permissions, Wipf and Stock Publishers, 199 W. 8th Ave., Suite 3, Eugene, OR 97401.

Wipf & Stock
An Imprint of Wipf and Stock Publishers
199 W. 8th Ave., Suite 3
Eugene, OR 97401

www.wipfandstock.com

PAPERBACK ISBN: 979-8-3852-3623-7
HARDCOVER ISBN: 979-8-3852-3624-4
EBOOK ISBN: 979-8-3852-3625-1

01/09/25

New Revised Standard Version Bible, copyright 1989, Division of Christian Education of the National Council of the Churches of Christ in the United States of America. Used by permission. All rights reserved.

Contents

Acknowledgments | vii

Introduction | ix

1 Signs of Hope in the Church | 1
2 Models for Creating Healthy Congregations | 27
3 Signs of Healthy Congregations: A 4 C's Relational Perspective | 52
4 Research Project | 77
5 Where Do We Go from Here? Guidelines for Creating Hopeful and Healthy Congregations | 96

About the Author | 111

Appendix 1: Research Design | 113

Appendix 2: Emails to Denominational Leaders | 121

Appendix 3: Denominational Leader Recurring Themes | 124

Appendix 4: Pastor Recurring Themes | 126

Appendix 5: Denominational Leader Questionnaire Responses | 128

Appendix 6: Pastor Questionnaires Responses | 130

Appendix 7: Four C's Questionnaires Responses | 132

Contents

Appendix 8: Case Study—Chapel by the Sea: Moclips/Pacific Beach, Washington | 134

Appendix 9: Case Study—First Presbyterian Church: Hastings, Nebraska | 142

Bibliography | 147

Acknowledgments

I AM DEEPLY GRATEFUL to the following people:

Members of two support groups, one personal and one professional, for their support and enthusiasm for this research and writing project.

Members of my family, especially my wife, Carol, and my children and their partners: Matt, Michele, Chris and Sam, and Juliann and Lawrence. Their ongoing interest in and wholehearted appreciation for my calling as a researcher and writer are deeply appreciated gifts!

Matthew Wimer and his Wipf and Stock editorial and publication teams, for their rare and unwavering commitment to publish books based on merit.

And especially the denominational leaders and pastors who participated in the research project on which this book is based. It is to them and their healthy and hopeful congregations that I dedicate this book.

Introduction

How hopeful are you about mainline churches at this point in the twenty-first century? For example, what are signs of hope that make your heart sing? How about signs of concern or disappointment that make your heart ache? Put another way, what are the conditions in which it seems hope thrives?

Then, too, how healthy do you think mainline churches are today? For example, what are the signs of vital, lively, thriving, or flourishing congregations?

These questions were put to five hundred denominational leaders in six mainline denominations: Episcopal and Lutheran bishops, United Church of Christ conference ministers, American Baptist executive ministers, Presbyterian executive presbyters, and United Methodist district superintendents.

Their answers may surprise you.

For example, denominational leaders are hopeful or very hopeful for over 80 percent of congregations in their regions, while they are not very hopeful for only 15 percent of their congregations.

Likewise, these denominational leaders believe 70 percent of congregations in their regions are healthy or very healthy, while only 20 percent are not very healthy.

There are also recurring themes about hope and health from these denominational leaders centered in *change, focus, leadership,* and *spiritual life*. For example, recurring themes about hopeful congregations include working together, being mission-focused,

Introduction

doing outreach, being willing to change, and nurturing spiritual life. Themes about least hopeful congregations include not being willing to change, being me-focused, providing weak leadership, and not nurturing spiritual life. Similarly, conditions in which hope thrives include providing strong leadership, being mission-focused, developing organizational life, and being willing to change. Finally, themes about healthy congregations include nurturing spiritual life, being mission-focused, providing strong leadership, doing outreach, and being willing to change

Now let's turn our attention to what these denominational leaders think hopeful and healthy churches do well. Hopeful congregations do well setting and meeting goals, energetically pursuing goals, and finding ways to solve problems even when discouraged.

Healthy congregations do well on a cross-section of markers, including providing leadership; anchoring their lives and ministries biblically and theologically; providing Christian formation; providing Spirit-inspired, thought-provoking worship; engaging in mission and outreach; welcoming new people; and achieving financial stability. They also do well in how they create community, communicate, treat one another, and work together.

***

In recent years there have been myriad ways to understand and describe healthy congregations. Whether healthy congregations are described in terms of themes, ways, signposts, characteristics, marks, experience, activities, factors, competencies, practices, principles, features, or priorities, most of these varying descriptions have three features in common: *relationships, leadership,* and *practices.*

From a relational perspective, in particular, where do you see signs of health in the church? In what areas of the church's relational life and ministry might we search for signs of health? When I think of places to look or search for words or concepts that best capture signs of relational health, this *four C's* framework comes to mind: *community, communication, character,* and *collaboration.*

Introduction

Community has to do with *ways we share with one another*, communication with *ways we interact with one another*, character with *ways we treat one another*, and collaboration with *ways we work with one another*.

What, though, are practical ways these four signs of relational health are exemplified? Here are six ways each is demonstrated:

Community

Building relationships
Affirming and supporting
Experiencing trust
Showing empathy
Practicing forgiveness
Bridging cultures

Communication

Engaging conflict
Listening attentively
Finding common ground
Technologically savvy
Expressing appreciation
Exercising curiosity

Character

Doing justice
Showing kindness
Practicing humility
Feeling compassion
Demonstrating love
Promoting peace

Collaboration

Strategizing and visioning
Discerning and decision-making
Openness to change
Organizational agility
Engagement of spiritual gifts
Partnering

Since denominational leaders were not able to assess how well congregations in their regions are doing in these practical aspects of community, communication, character, and collaboration, they identified several churches in their regions for which they are most hopeful and which are most healthy. In fact, they identified over one hundred such churches to gain further, more in-depth information. Pastors of these churches provide an in-depth look at hope and health in their congregations.

As with denominational leaders, some of their assessments may surprise you.

INTRODUCTION

Perhaps counterintuitively, while pastors of hopeful congregations believe their congregations are slightly more hopeful than healthy, pastors of healthy congregations believe their congregations are considerably more hopeful than healthy, and pastors of both hopeful and healthy congregations believe they are considerably more healthy than hopeful.

Recurring themes about hope and health from these pastors also center on *change, focus, and spiritual life*, although *working together* replaces leadership. In fact, spiritual life, mission-focused, and working together are the top three signs of both hope and health. Willingness to change and outreach are also prominent.

Like their denominational leaders, while pastors of hopeful and healthy congregations believe their congregations do most things well, they do nothing either poorly or exceptionally well. More specifically, as with denominational leaders, pastors believe their congregations do well on all seven measures of congregational health.

All four C's are done well as signs of health with character and collaboration at the top of the list for pastors and character and community for denominational leaders. Communication is rated lowest for both. Perhaps most significantly, all twenty-four practical ways our four signs of health are exemplified are done well or fairly well.

OVERVIEW OF THIS BOOK

You'll find five chapters in this book.

Chapter 1, "Signs of Hope in the Church," presents four core beliefs about hope:

- The future will be better than the present.
- We have the power to make it so.
- There are many paths to our goals.
- None of our goals are free from obstacles.

It also offers these seven guidelines for making hope happen:

INTRODUCTION

- Think of hope as biblically anchored.
- Link truth and hope.
- Link hope and faith.
- Face global, systemic crises and change with active hope.
- Link mission and hope to create change.
- Think of hope as having a realistic goal along with the will and the way to accomplish it.
- Hope matters and is a choice we can learn to make and share with others.

Chapter 2, "Models for Creating Healthy Congregations," identifies eighteen conceptions of healthy congregations over the last four decades. Six are research-based, five denomination-based, five book-based, and two are classified as "others."

Chapter 3, "Signs of Healthy Congregations: A 4 C's Relational Perspective," presents a new, fully developed framework for understanding relational health in mainline churches. An important question remains: how are our congregations doing in each of the practical ways they create community, communicate, treat one another, and work together? We assess the validity of these signs of healthy congregations as measures of relational health in the research project outlined in the next chapter, chapter 4.

Chapter 4, "Research Project," presents an empirical test of the validity and usefulness of our core beliefs about hope, our cross-section of signs of health in mainline churches, and our new relational approach to congregational health in mainline churches. Included are this research project's design, results, observations and discussion, and conclusions.

Chapter 5, "Where Do We Go from Here? Guidelines for Creating Hopeful and Healthy Congregations," offers reflections on how mainline churches may move into a more hope-filled and healthy future.

You will find practical application study guides and suggestions for further study. Further resources include chapter footnotes, appendices, and a bibliography at the back of the book.

Introduction

In summary, this book features heretofore unknown assessments and surprising findings about the hope and health of twenty-first-century mainline churches from the perspectives of their denominational leaders and pastors. Perhaps it is time to replace our lament over problems facing twenty-first-century mainline churches with aspirations of hope and possibilities for health!

1

Signs of Hope in the Church

What oxygen is for the lungs, such is hope for the meaning of human life.
—Emil Brunner

The capacity for hope is the most significant fact of life. It provides human beings with a sense of destination and the energy to get started.
—Norman Cousins

For surely I know the plans I have for you, says the Lord, plans for your welfare and not for harm, to give you a future with hope.
—Jeremiah 29:11

My parents had the typical expectations and dreams for me and my siblings that most parents have for their children—hopes for our safety, our happiness, and overall wellbeing. However, life has a way of turning some parental dreams into disappointment, if not outright nightmarish detours. Such was the case with my parents when, as a toddler just learning to walk, I received serious burns on all my fingers from accidentally putting them on the top of our woodburning stove. After being rushed to the hospital and treated for my burns, I was outfitted with protective metal shields on each finger. My parents were sure that their failure to protect me from harm would severely delay my learning to walk. Fortunately, their worst fears and dreams for my safety and wellbeing did not materialize as the metal shields ended up aiding my balance and not delaying my ability to walk after all.

Fast-forward to my early childhood years and the hopes my parents had for me in learning to experience trust. My parents took several actions that left indelible positive memories in my trust formation. One such action was in giving me a hatchet on my fourth or fifth birthday. My father was a logger during those years, and so learning to use such a potentially dangerous toy at such an early age was not unheard of in my household. Fortunately, their trust in my capacity to safely handle the hatchet was well-placed as I still have all my fingers. Also, at a noticeably early age, my parents trusted me to stay away from a dangerous open pit well at the back of our yard by not crossing a rope they placed around it. This trust-enhancing experience is also deeply imprinted in my memory bank as a fond and influential childhood moment in time.

These memorable and influential childhood experiences demonstrate an important distinction between our dreams and fantasies and our hopes. Dreams and expectations remain wishful thinking unless action is taken to accomplish them. My parents took specific steps to make their hopes for my wellbeing happen. We have the power to make the future better than the present. That is exactly what guided my parents' child-rearing practices even when their hopes were derailed. As renown hope researcher Shane J. Lopez puts it, we create the future we want for ourselves and others by making hope happen.[1] Hope is a way of thinking that requires effort to accomplish goals we set for ourselves, including finding pathways around obstacles that stand in our way. As Lopez points out, "We reinforce our capacity for hope each time we

---

1. See Lopez, *Making Hope Happen*, 11.

experiment with problem-solving strategies and persist until one works."[2] Moreover, Lopez comments, "This type of thinking about the future gives us momentum and staying power. The sustained energy we devote to our most important goals represents another crucial way in which hope parts company with plain old positive thinking."[3] In short, we've discovered these four core beliefs about hope:[4]

- The future will be better than the present.
- We have the power to make it so.
- There are many paths to our goals.
- None of our goals are free from obstacles.

While privileged people do not have a corner on hope, it is often the case that those without hope have barriers to overcome that make the likelihood of making hope happen more challenging and difficult, if not impossible in some instances. At times, people can't simply pull themselves up by their own bootstraps without assistance. Rather, they need the benefit of a helping hand. Moreover, as Isabel Wilkerson wisely notes in her Pulitzer Prize winning book *Caste: The Origins of Our Discontents*, "The price of privilege is the moral duty to act when one sees another person treated unfairly. And the least that a person in the dominant caste can do is not make the pain any worse."[5] More will be said about this point later in this chapter and in chapter 3.

In this chapter, you'll find seven guidelines of practical wisdom for making hope happen in the everyday life of our congregations, homes, work life, and society. Also, look for best practices gleaned from recent research for how making hope happen transforms our life on planet earth for the better.

---

2. Lopez, *Making Hope Happen*, 19.
3. Lopez, *Making Hope Happen*, 19.
4. Lopez, *Making Hope Happen*, 18–19.
5. Wilkerson, *Caste*, 386.

GUIDELINES FOR MAKING HOPE HAPPEN

1. Think of Hope as Biblically Anchored

What hopes do you have for the church these days? What makes your heart sing? Alternatively, what concerns you about the church? What makes your heart ache? These questions frame our exploration of and quest for signs of hope in the church. Christian hope grows out of the biblical meaning of hope: to wait patiently or to wait in confident expectation. Without expectation, despair can arise. And the waiting is usually upon God. Moreover, "if hope is fixed on God, it embraces at once the three elements of expectation of the future, trust, and the patience of waiting."[6] More specifically, we may wait patiently and confidently for God's gift of salvation. "Thus Christian hope rests on the divine act of salvation accomplished in Christ, and, since this is eschatological, hope itself is an eschatological blessing, i.e., now is the time when we may have confidence."[7] As Paul puts it in 2 Cor 3:4, "Such is the confidence that we have through Christ toward God." And notice that this confidence has an active dimension comparable to making hope happen. Patience and persistence are involved. For example, we are told in 1 Pet 1:13, "Therefore prepare your minds for action; discipline yourselves; set all your hope on the grace that Jesus Christ will bring you when he is revealed." And as Paul goes on to write in 2 Cor 3:12, "Since, then, we have such a hope, we act with great boldness." The writer of the Letter to the Hebrews in 6:11–12 makes similar reference to an active hope: "And we want each one of you to show the same diligence so as to realize the full assurance of hope to the very end, so that you may not become sluggish, but imitators of those who through faith and patience inherit the promises." Additionally, we find the notion of a "living hope" in 1 Pet 1:3, and in Jer 29:11, we find this aspiration: "For surely I know the plans I have for you, says the Lord, plans for your welfare and not for harm, to give you a future with hope."

---

6. Kittel, *Theological Dictionary*, 531.
7. Kittel, *Theological Dictionary*, 532.

Similarly, in Isa 40:31, we find these benefits of active hope: "But those who wait for the LORD shall renew their strength, they shall mount up with wings like eagles, they shall run and not be weary, they shall walk and not faint."

In *God of the Oppressed*, American Methodist minister and theologian James Cone helpfully makes this point with respect to the link between hope and justice: "How can Christian theology truly speak of the hope of Jesus Christ, unless that hope begins and ends with the liberation of the poor in the social existence in which theology takes shape? In America this means that there can be no talk about hope in the Christian sense unless it is talk about the freedom of black, red, and brown people."[8] In fact, Cone connects hope in Jesus with human suffering, freedom, and liberation. He goes on to say, "Because Black Theology's Christology is based on the biblical portrayal of Jesus Christ and Jesus' past and present involvement in the struggle of oppressed peoples, it affirms that who Jesus Christ is for us today is connected with the divine future as disclosed in the liberation fight of the poor. When connected with the person of Jesus, hope is not an intellectual idea; rather, it is the praxis of freedom in the oppressed community."[9] He concludes, "To hope in Jesus is to see the vision of his coming presence, and thus one is required by hope itself to live as if the vision is already realized in the present."[10]

In *Postcolonial Imagination and Feminist Theology*, Professor of Christian Theology and Spirituality Kwok Pui-lan makes a similar point with respect to Third World and Indigenous women. She writes, "Women of color's eschatological hope is grounded in their continual struggle and resistance, creating new resources for survival. A reconnection with one's cultural and spiritual traditions does not mean romanticizing the past, nor overlooking the fact that one's culture has been transformed and appropriated in the political and spiritual conquest by the West. Rather, what is under way is a lifelong process of searching for cultural and spiritual

---

8. Cone, *God of the Oppressed*, 117.
9. Cone, *God of the Oppressed*, 118.
10. Cone, *God of the Oppressed*, 118–19.

resources to live by in a world dominated by white supremacy, capitalist greed, and patriarchy. This is an effort to create a way out of no way."[11] In *Postcolonial Politics and Theology*, she goes on to say, "Postcolonial hope is not a dream but a praxis. It is not passive waiting but an active pursuit of justice. The author of Hebrews summons us, surrounded by this great cloud of witnesses, to 'run with perseverance the race that is set before us, looking to Jesus the pioneer and perfector of our faith' (Heb 12:1). As Jesus resisted the Roman Empire in his time, so too must we refuse to be pawns of mighty empires, standing up to state violence and police brutality, challenging myths and lies, and making grieving a revolutionary practice."[12]

2. Link Truth and Hope

Hebrew Bible scholar and contemporary prophetic voice Walter Brueggemann suggests that there can be no hope without truth being told. He comments, "Our temptation, of course, is to do the work of hope without the prior work of truth."[13] Brueggemann sees this sequence as theologically rooted: "Truth-telling is grounded in the God who will not be mocked by our illusions. Hope is God-grounded in the conviction that even our wayward resistance does not negate God's good resolve for fidelity in the creation of futures. Without that God-groundedness, truth-telling can readily become nothing more than harping, and hope-telling only wishful thinking."[14] More specifically, like Cone and Kwok Pui-lan, Brueggemann points out that, in our Christian tradition, the sequence of truth and hope is highlighted in the Friday of Jesus's crucifixion and the Sunday of Jesus's resurrection: "The Friday crucifixion of Jesus amounts to truth-telling against the Roman Empire—namely, that the lethal capacity of Rome can do its work,

---

11. Kwok, *Postcolonial Imagination*, 228.
12. Kwok, *Postcolonial Politics*, 202–3.
13. Brueggemann, *Truth and Hope*, xiv.
14. Brueggemann, *Truth and Hope*, xiv.

but it is not enough and will not bring wellbeing. And so Sunday is a dramatic embodiment of hope for the power of life over the scandal of death. And of course in church practice we would like to do the hope of Easter without the truth of Good Friday, as witnessed in the contrast in church attendance on those days."[15] And finally, Brueggemann makes explicit the church's contemporary context and task for this link between truth and hope: "To tell the truth about the way in which our dominant way of consumer militarism (under the guise of American exceptionalism) will fail, because it contradicts the purposes of God, and to tell the hope that God is at work for an alternative world of peace with justice."[16]

In *Caste*, Isabel Wilkerson illustrates the importance of facing the truth by describing how the inhumanity that is the Holocaust has become part of the German peoples' DNA. She comments, "This fact, this history, is built into the consciousness of Berliners as they go about their everyday lives. It is not something that anyone, Jew or Gentile, resident or visitor, is expected to put behind them or to just get over. They do not run from it. It has become a part of who they are because it is a part of what they have been. They incorporate it into their identity because it is, in fact, them."[17] And then there's the guilt and shame that must also be faced and experienced in dealing with the awful atrocities. Moreover, there's the necessity of remembering this history so that it is never repeated. *Facing the truth, feeling shame, and remembering*, then, are vital elements in dealing with the Holocaust and such other historical atrocities as slavery in America. In addition, there are *reparations or restitution* that have been rightly paid and continue to be paid to survivors of the Holocaust—something Congress has considered for victims of slavery in America but has heretofore failed to pass legislation to make a reality. Finally, there is the *responsibility* of ongoing generations. Here is how Wilkerson reports the reaction of German students on tours of the history of the Third Reich: "We are Germans, and Germans perpetrated this. . . . And, though it

---

15. Brueggemann, *Truth and Hope*, xiv.
16. Brueggemann, *Truth and Hope*, xiv.
17. Wilkerson, *Caste*, 348.

wasn't just Germans, it is the older Germans who were here who should feel guilt. We were not here. We ourselves did not do this. But we do feel that, as the younger generation, we should acknowledge and accept the responsibility. And for the generations that come after us, we should be the guardians of the truth."[18]

3. Link Hope and Faith

Influential German theologian Jurgen Moltmann suggests that hope is the *inseparable companion* of faith. In his groundbreaking work *Theology of Hope*, he comments, "Faith is the foundation upon which hope rests, hope nourishes and sustains faith."[19] Moltmann continues, "Without hope, faith falls to pieces, becomes a fainthearted and ultimately a dead faith. It is through faith that [humankind] finds the path of true life, but it is only hope that keeps [us] on that path. Thus it is that faith in Christ gives hope its assurance. Thus it is that hope gives faith in Christ its breadth and leads it into life."[20] Similarly, in Moltmann's recent work, *The Spirit of Hope*, he says simply, "Faith and hope are reciprocally related,"[21] citing John Calvin's comment, "Faith is the foundation on which hope rests, but it is hope that keeps faith upright and alive."[22] Faith, then, depends on hope for its life. Hope activates faith, reminding us of James's assertion that faith without works is dead.[23] Likewise, Professor of Theology Damayanhui N. A. Niles comments in *Hope for the World: Mission in a Global Context*, "Although hope is transcendent it must be embodied and enacted in this world."[24]

---

18. Wilkerson, *Caste*, 348.
19. Moltmann, *Theology of Hope*, 20.
20. Moltmann, *Theology of Hope*, 20.
21. Moltmann, *Spirit of Hope*, 142.
22. See Moltmann, *Spirit of Hope*, 142n7.
23. See Jas 2:17, 26.
24. Niles, "Common Hope," 107.

4. Face Global Systemic Crises and Change with Active Hope

While not a primary focus of this book, it is worth noting that Moltmann in *The Spirit of Hope* suggests that hope helps us face a world in crisis and peril, particularly such global challenges as social and economic inequality, climate change, and terrorism. He brings hope to bear in our profoundly troubled and despairing times with reflections on such topics as the ecological challenge, interfaith relations, solidarity and compassion, and terrorism in the name of religion.[25] These reflections identify what we can learn from the past and offer wise commentary for facing the future. Let's examine just a little more specifically some of our current global systemic change and challenges and consider the way active hope helps us face them.

Louis Stulman in his foreword to *Truth and Hope* notes these alarming seismic shifts in our cultural, political, and religious milieu in the early 2020s:[26]

- Deepening fissures in American culture, unprecedented in our lifetime
- The rejection of democratic norms
- The resurgence of white nationalism
- The dismantling of civic discourse and civil society
- A greater tolerance of racial bigotry
- Horrifying gun violence in schools
- Dehumanization of immigrants, even the seizure of children from parents at the border
- Increasing economic disparities
- Assaults against woman's rights, environmental protections, the judiciary, and the free press
- Contempt for truth

25. See Moltmann, *Spirit of Hope*, vii.
26. Stulman, in *Truth and Hope*, ix.

- Disturbing alliances of Christian communions with autocratic political systems
- Disillusionment with long-standing forms of religious life, especially among millennials
- Resultant widespread despair and palpable cynicism

Against this backdrop, there are signs of hope in the church. "Hope is active, transformative conduct,"[27] asserts Brueggemann. Stulman cites these examples:[28]

> Already emerging from the wreckage are signs of resistance, creativity, and empowerment. We are witnessing grassroots movements with renewed commitments to the teachings of Jesus, communities confronting animus toward Muslims, sexual violence, and the dehumanization of refugees and minorities. In this fight for "the soul of the nation and the integrity of faith," a number of community leaders are confronting "the resurgence of white nationalism, racism, and xenophobia; misogyny; attacks on immigrants, refugees, and the poor; the regular purveying of falsehoods and consistent lying by the nation's highest leaders; and moves toward autocratic political leadership and authoritarian rule."

Future earth is a global network of scientists, researchers, and innovators collaborating for a more sustainable planet. Their 2020 report of Global Risks Perceptions Survey (GRPS) results reveals the top five global risks identified by over two hundred global change scientists from fifty-two countries. These risks include climate change, extreme weather, biodiversity loss, food crises, and water crises.[29] Global risks are defined as uncertain events or conditions that, if they occur, can cause significant negative impacts for several countries or industries within the next ten years. These natural, social, and human scientists believe these risks can lead

---

27. Bruggemann, *Truth and Hope*, 127.

28. Stulman, in *Truth and Hope*, x. Stulman in this note cites the "Reclaiming Jesus Statement," http://www.reclaimingjesus.org.

29. See Future Earth, Risks Perceptions Report 2020.

to a global systemic crisis: "Together these five risks threaten the continued integrity of the biosphere and its capacity to support itself and human life. This collective perspective underscores the crucial need to consider societal risks and environmental risks jointly rather than in isolation."[30] And to address this growing existential threat to our planet and humanity, these global change scientists suggest that "we need to open dialogue on risk to a diversity of voices, allowing us to assess a complex issue from multiple perspectives. Ultimately, we strive to enrich our understanding of risks through dialogue and to move the global narrative towards common solutions. We hope this report, and future iterations, will help move us forward on this path."[31]

The 2021 Future earth GRPS report results on the top five global risks identified by over two hundred global change scientists from all fields and disciplines in over sixty-five countries include failure to take climate action, biodiversity loss, infectious disease, extreme weather events, and human environmental damage.[32] Environmental risks were ranked among the most urgent global risks humanity faces today and as highly interconnected with other global risks (societal, economic, geopolitical, and technical). Technological risks are now seen as more likely to occur compared to earlier findings. Scientists highlighted the need to prioritize inequality as a standalone risk.

The 2023 Global Risks Report of the World Economic Forum, an international organization for public-private cooperation, ranks global risks by severity over the short term (two years) and long term (ten years). Its 2023 GRPS results from over 1200 experts across academia, business, government, the international community, and civil society rank the top five short term risks as cost-of-living crisis, natural disasters and extreme weather events, geoeconomic confrontation, failure to mitigate climate change, and erosion of social cohesion and societal polarization. The top five long-term risks are failure to mitigate climate change, failure of

30. Future Earth, Risks Perceptions Report 2020, 1.
31. Future Earth, Risks Perceptions Report 2020, 1.
32. See Future Earth, Global Risks Perceptions Report 2021.

climate-change adaptation, natural disasters and extreme weather events, biodiversity loss and ecosystem collapse, and large-scale involuntary migration.[33] According to Saadia Zahidi, managing director of the World Economic Forum, "The 2023 edition of the Global Risks Report highlights the multiple areas where the world is at a critical inflection point. It is a call to action, to collectively prepare for the next crisis the world may face and, in doing so, shape a pathway to a more stable, resilient world."[34]

While we've identified these global risk challenges and changes, we're left with this important question: how are we to face our growing global systemic crisis? Ecophilosopher Joanna Macy and physician Chris Johnstone recommend that active hope is our best option. In their recent book *Active Hope: How to Face the Mess We're in with Resilience and Creative Power*, Macy and Johnstone suggest that, rather than feel overwhelmed and do nothing or feel satisfied with and resigned to the way things are, active hope "involves identifying the outcomes we hope for and then playing a role in moving toward them."[35] They recommend four steps in the pathway of active hope: *gratitude* with love and appreciation for what sustains us; *honoring our pain for the world* by looking at the future we're heading into and naming our concerns; *seeing with new eyes* by seeking inspiration for facing these concerns and deciding what we hope for as we face the future; and *going forth* with the part we'd like to play in the activation of our hope. Gratitude grounds and strengthens our capacity to face present realities; honoring our pain activates our feelings of connection, caring, and compassion; seeing with new eyes widens our vision, expands our collaborative resources, and focuses our hope; and going forth offers our energy, motivation, support, and actions on behalf of life on planet earth.

---

33. See World Economic Forum Global Risks, Global Risks Perception Survey 2022–2023.

34. World Economic Forum Global Risks, Global Risks Perception Survey 2022–2023, 4.

35. Macy and Johnstone, *How to Face the Mess*, 41.

5. Link Mission and Hope to Create Change

Congregational systems consultant Peter Steinke in *A Door Set Open: Grounding Change in Mission and Hope* suggests that "hope puts possibility into play. Hope is a concrete invitation to act in adventurous ways."[36] He has discovered that mission and hope are related to navigating inevitable changes and challenges facing the church such that "changes are connected to mission and sustained by hope."[37] Among his observations of how best to manage the challenge of change are the following:[38]

- Transformation involves crisis.
- Without mature and motivated leaders, little happens.
- Clergy are not well prepared to conduct the change process.
- How emotional processes are understood and handled plays a major role in outcomes.
- Resistance to change is far less intense and protracted when change is made for the sake of mission.
- People are motivated by both pain and hope.
- Congregations can be trapped in the status quo because they are fundamentally unaware of how societal change has affected the local parish.
- People will be more receptive to ideas that are solidly grounded in Scripture and theology.
- Good intentions are fortified by good planning and action.

Steinke helpfully contrasts hopefulness with hopelessness in the following ways:[39]

- Hopefulness stirs imagination whereas hopelessness shrinks the radius of possibility.

---

36. Steinke, *Door Set Open*, 3.
37. Steinke, *Door Set Open*, 122.
38. Steinke, *Door Set Open*, 2.
39. Steinke, *Door Set Open*, 41.

- Hopefulness has the capacity to wait while hopelessness becomes restless or apathetic.
- Hopefulness expands horizons while hopelessness minimizes options.
- Hopefulness creates a sense of buoyancy while hopelessness loses heart and spirit.
- Hopefulness looks for help outside while hopelessness withdraws from interaction.

Steinke believes with family-systems expert Edwin Friedman that the way leaders handle people's resistance is at the heart of effective ministry and positive change: "The capacity of a leader to be aware of, to reflect upon, and to work through people's reactivity may be the most important aspect of leadership. It is 'the key to the kingdom.'"[40] Moreover, Steinke states, "The challenge of change for leaders is to keep one's eye on the ball (stay focused), take the heat (remain nonreactive), stay connected (talk and listen), and get a good night's sleep."[41]

6. *Think of Hope as Having a Realistic Goal Along with the Will and the Way to Accomplish It*

Hope research by social scientists gives us insight and practical direction in our quest for signs of hope in the church and our search for places to look for signs of hope. Social scientists define hope as the ability to create pathways for accomplishing desired goals and the motivation to make use of those pathways.[42] Psychologist C. R. Snyder, pioneer hope researcher, suggests that hope is goal-directed and requires willpower and "waypower."[43] The saying "where there's a will there's a way" doesn't work in creating hope. Rather, both the will and the way are required to accomplish

---

40. Steinke, *Door Set Open*, 119–20.
41. Steinke, *Door Set Open*, 121.
42. See Rand and Cheavens, *Oxford Handbook of Positive Psychology*, 323.
43. See Snyder, *Psychology of Hope*, 10.

the goals we hope to accomplish. Attempts to lose weight illustrate this point. If we hope to lose weight, we must first set a realistic weight loss goal. Next, we must decide that we really want to do so. It takes goal-setting and determination to lose weight. However, having the will to lose weight without knowing how to go about doing so is likely to result in failure. Besides determination and persistence, we also must select a weight loss plan or pathway to accomplish our goal, knowing there will be obstacles we'll need to confront along the way. In short, our hope to accomplish our weight loss goal will remain a dream without determination (the will) and strategy (the way).

Moreover, rather than defining hope in terms of behaviors, emotions, self-esteem, intelligence, or previous achievements, Snyder links hope to potential success in reaching one's goals. He also created a useful Hope Scale to measure our hope mindset based on the degree to which we:[44]

- energetically pursue our goals.
- can think of many ways to get out of a jam.
- use past experiences to prepare for our future.
- find many ways to solve problems.
- are successful in life.
- can think of many ways to get what we want out of life.
- meet goals we set for ourselves.
- find solutions to problems even when others get discouraged.

Early childhood and adolescent experiences often are influential in making hope happen, as we saw in the opening scenarios. Snyder provides practical tips for developing hopeful thinking goals, waypower, and willpower. Here are some "do's" and "don't's" for nurturing hope in children:[45]

---

44. Snyder, *Psychology of Hope*, 26.
45. Snyder, *Psychology of Hope*, 176–77, 189–90, and 204–5. For a similar set of tips kindling hope in adults, see pages 223–24, 239–40, and 254.

Goal-Setting Tips

- Listen to their wants, help them identify their desires, and show interest in their goals.
- Help them match their goals with their talents.
- Don't second-guess their goals or push them to set extremely difficult goals.

Willpower Tips

- Inspire self-determination and focus more on strengths than weaknesses.
- Help them face roadblocks with patience and a sense of humor.
- Support their efforts without solving their problems or telling them how to proceed.

Waypower Tips

- Teach them how things work and build their academic, social, and decision-making skills.
- Discuss plans for reaching their goals and how to break down goals into doable steps.
- Don't tire of "why" questions or stop answering them, and don't minimize their concerns.

For an excellent educational resource to help students apply hope theory for goal-setting, maintaining motivation, and overcoming obstacles, see professor of psychology Jeana L. Magyar-Moe's creative learning activity, "Hope Projects to One's Future Self."[46]

---

46. See Magyar-Moe, *Activities in Teaching Positive Psychology*, 137–42.

7. Hope Matters and Is a Choice We Can Learn to Make and Share with Others

American journalist Norman Cousins makes this bold assertion: "The capacity for hope is the most significant fact of life. It provides human beings with a sense of destination and the energy to get started." From his research and clinical practice, psychologist Shane Lopez concludes simply, "We can't live without hope."[47] In fact, suggests Lopez, "How we think about the future—*how we hope*—determines how well we live our lives."[48] For example, hope research finds that higher hope corresponds with superior academic and athletic performance, greater physical and psychological wellbeing, and enhanced interpersonal relationships.[49] More specifically, hope research has now established that high-hope people have higher grades, workplace performance, and overall wellbeing than their low-hope counterparts.[50] Research also finds that high-hope people live happier lives, have better health, live longer, are more dependable workers, and are more productive than low-hope individuals.[51]

So, hope matters! As theologian Emil Brunner comments, "What oxygen is for the lungs, such is hope for the meaning of human life." Fortunately, hope is a choice we make: it can be learned, and it can be shared with others. Let's examine these three features of making hope happen.

Choosing to Hope

It is especially challenging to choose to hope in the face of fear. Fear helps us face threatening, stressful, or risky situations by escaping what scares us. We put blinders on and concentrate on finding the most obvious way to escape when we are afraid. Hope,

---

47. Lopez, *Making Hope Happen*, 10 (emphasis original).
48. Lopez, *Making Hope Happen*, 9.
49. See Rand and Cheavens, *Oxford Handbook of Positive Psychology*, 323.
50. See Lopez, *Making Hope Happen*, 50–51.
51. See Lopez, *Making Hope Happen*, 51–61.

on the other hand, requires us to take off our blinders to see the opportunities for getting where we want to go in risky or stressful situations. As Lopez suggests, "We have more pathways to the future when hope edges out fear. Innovation comes out of hope; we create something out of nothing, then tweak, tweak, tweak until it works just right. Hope works because it broadens our thinking *and* because it fuels persistence. Big thinking without stick-to-itiveness is not hoping, it's wishing."[52] It's a balancing act: managing fear and choosing hope.

Thus far, we've seen that hope matters and that it is a choice we make. How, though, do we learn to hope?

Learning to Hope

All of us preview the future every day. We get up in the morning and check the weather. We take medications to safeguard our health. We glance at our schedule to see what we need to do during the day. To help us learn which goals to future-cast, it helps to dedicate ourselves to goals that we are excited about, align with our strengths, and make a significant impact on ourselves and others.

Next, it helps to put our brains on autopilot by creating triggers to activate our goals. We all need protection from that which pulls us off course and warning signs when something is amiss. For example, we place our iPhone on a nightstand as a trigger to remind us to check the weather each morning when we get out of bed. We put our medications on the bathroom counter in a container with dosages for each day of the week to save time and to trigger us not to forget to take our medications as prescribed. And we trigger our memory as to what we'll do that day from glancing at the planning calendar we left next to the place mat where we'll have breakfast so that we lessen the chance that we'll overlook or fail to attend an important meeting at work. All these prompts or cues help us tap into the energy we need to successfully pursue our goals.

---

52. Lopez, *Making Hope Happen*, 113.

Finally, we can anticipate obstacles and create multiple pathways to each of our goals. Remember: there are often many paths to our goals, and none of them is free of obstacles. Among the tactics we can use in planning for "ifs" are facing our fears, thinking about alternatives, building on strengths, meeting needs, and borrowing hope from others. Consider these examples.

We can win the victory of facing our fear of bees if we check out the logistics of picnic area options in local parks that are likely to not attract bees in the first place.

We can learn to think about alternative pathways. For instance, workers need freedom to fail and learn to overcome troubles they encounter. They can be taught to think about strategies to solve problems, thereby raising their level of hope for being successful at work.

Building pathways from strengths is an effective way for teachers to help students raise their hopes for doing well in school. Many of us have a lower view of ourselves than we should have because we've learned to focus on what we don't do well instead of building on our strengths. For instance, why is it that we get a math quiz back with minus-three circled in red ink? If our teacher had instead returned our quiz with plus-twenty-seven circled in green ink, we'd have had a more accurate view of our math skills.

Meeting community needs such as more adequate housing brings hope for homeless neighbors when a city council decides to invest in the construction of tiny houses to be located on unused portions of church properties in the community.

Likewise, our hope that children will learn what we wish to teach them is increased if our subject matter is linked to a meaningful product or outcome. For example, the need for junior high students to be motivated to learn to sing is enhanced if they have a say in selecting the music and then have fun preparing a concert to entertain their families and classmates. It turns their rehearsal work into an enjoyable and worthwhile musical experience for all.

Sometimes, though, we've faced our fears, explored all alternatives, built on our strengths, and met needs—and we still come up short on the resources we need to create and sustain hope. What would happen, though, if our needs become known to caring others? We can borrow hope from them. Examples include finding mentors, contacting nonprofit-funding sources, networking with people with similar interests, and receiving goodwill of well-intentioned community members and volunteer organizations. My wife struggled with a learning disability that limited her writing ability to be successful in her graduate program. She needed an editor for her paperwork—skills that I had and willingly offered to her. She also needed understanding professors who were willing to find creative ways for her to complete and pass her exams. They agreed to call on her in class only if she raised her hand. They let her take exams in a room by herself, without the pressure of time limits, and then graded her on what she was able to complete. She borrowed from their understanding, goodwill, and problem-solving creativity to find alternate ways to demonstrate her knowledge and competencies.

These examples illustrate the importance and value of putting into practice Isabel Wilkerson's "price of privilege" mentioned earlier in this chapter. Learned educators joined me in exercising our moral duty and responsibility to act when we saw another person suffering the legacy of undiagnosed learning disabilities early in life. We created a fair and equitable way for my wife to succeed in graduate school when she would have continued to struggle and possibly fail academically without our creative and helpful interventions. We empowered her to complete her graduate studies and to live into her hope of becoming a pastor. It helped make her hope happen!

Sharing Hope

We can each create ripples of hope that make our personal hope a public resource. It can help solve our biggest societal problems and make our communities better. Let's examine how sharing hope can make hope happen for others.

First, we can lead with hope. Team members need hope. Whether it is team leaders at work, church, school, or in the community, research indicates that followers look to their leaders to meet four psychological needs: trust, stability, compassion, and hope,[53] and in return, team members promise their trust, creativity, commitment, and engagement.[54] How, though, do our leaders make hope happen and help us create a better future?

Lopez suggests that leaders who want to spread hope and motivate their team practice three tactics: create excitement about the future, overcome obstacles, and reestablish goals when needed.[55] Let's consider each of these tactics, each of which we saw demonstrated by the educators who helped my wife succeed in graduate school.

Excitement

Team leaders who get workers involved and inspire enthusiasm about the future generate greater worker commitment and energy than that of disengaged coworkers. They are more productive, healthy, and permanent than their coworkers. Leaders fire them up by letting them do what they do best and want to make their lives better. They consistently offer positive feedback and calm encouragement. They are supportive and flexible. They create a safe work environment wherein communication builds trust and stability, and supportiveness diminishes defensiveness. They promote bold initiatives and the freedom to learn from failure. Everyone feels appreciated and part of the organization's success.

Obstacles

Hopeful leaders make our lives better and easier. When leaders remove obstacles to goals, they offer people opportunity to do their best. Like the educators in my wife's case, they give people options, draw attention to progress toward a goal, spark enthusiasm,

---

53. See Lopez, *Making Hope Happen*, 178.
54. Lopez, *Making Hope Happen*, 178.
55. Lopez, *Making Hope Happen*, 179.

and provide necessary resources to be successful. The city of Seattle received a sixty-eight-acre donation of prime real estate. A forward-thinking and process-savvy mayor appointed a citizen advisory committee to work with city planners to generate and evaluate options for using the land. Citizen input was taken seriously and enthusiastically by city leaders, resulting in initial land usage options drawing favorable community support and hope for a brighter future.

Reestablish Goals

Leading with hope is easy when the chances of being successful are high. Not so, though, when the chance of failure feels overwhelming. Hope requires courageous action to change course midstream—to *regoal*—despite cries of protest from those who delude themselves and cling to goals that are no longer viable or realistic. We may reconsider previous goals, find new stakeholders, revise or reestablish goals based on what is probable and possible, or let go of some of our dreams to build an updated version of the future and make our best potential future a reality. One congregation confronted an uncertain future due to dwindling financial resources and leadership energy. It became stuck in hopes for the future that had served them well in the past but were not able to move them into a better future. When the congregation failed to regoal, their hope for a better future waned. Eventually, the congregation reached a point where it was no longer viable, and it decided to close its doors.

A second way of sharing hope is to connect young people to a believable future by being a caring, hopeful adult, and by being excited by something in their future. For example, we can teach children to link current circumstances to their future, including helping them discover a variety of paths to meaningful goals.

Some students today feel as though their K–12 education does not address a "felt need."

For example, they don't make a connection between what they are learning in school and a career or future job. One way to connect students of all ages to their future is to help students view their current education as an investment in their future. Career days, mentoring, internships, "firsthand" learning projects, financial aid seminars, and earlier visits to higher-education schools are all effective if these activities help students create excitement and motivation about a job or career path. Such linkage between their current education and an exciting future creates a "felt need" and the valuation of hard work as a worthwhile investment in their future.

Once students have the will to work hard to create an exciting future, they still need to discover ways to activate their hope. They must learn how to get good grades, solve obstacles, and develop strategies required to reach their future goals. They'll need to think flexibly and create alternate pathways to reach their goals to match their wills with their ways to an exciting future.

Two final ways of sharing hope are to model hope and to build a network of hope for our friends, congregations, schools, workplaces, and communities. For example, we can model hope by offering a word of appreciation or praise that encourages others to do likewise. Watching colleagues at work go for a walk during their lunch break inspires us to begin exercising regularly. Seeing a parent order fruit instead of ice cream for their children at a fast-food restaurant signals to others the importance of healthy eating habits. And then noticing people's feelings of sadness or perplexity can prime us to model speaking words of encouragement, offering a listening ear or even just a supportive smile. Likewise, watching a nightly news broadcast of a touching human-interest story, going to movies about overcoming social injustice or human suffering, or reading books with inspiring stories or characters are examples of everyday models for connecting us to networks of hope.

Neighbors helping neighbors in times of trouble or struggle is an example of a network of caring people that offers hope and support. It may be comfort when facing the death of a friend or family member, coping strategies for the unexpected loss of a job, help in dealing with a pending retirement, safety from an abusive partner, or creative alternatives for managing an interpersonal conflict at home, church, school, or work.

SUMMARY

Seven guidelines for making hope happen are presented in chapter 1. We started with the realization that Christian hope grows out of our biblical understanding of hope. We then learned that there can be no hope without truth being told. Next, we learned that faith and hope are reciprocally related. Then we saw that hope helps us face global challenges. We also were reminded that changes and challenges facing the church are connected to mission and sustained by hope. From social science research, we gained insights that hope is goal-directed and requires both willpower and waypower. And finally, we learned both that we cannot live without hope, and that hope is a choice we make, can be learned, and can be shared with others.

In the chapter that follows, chapter 2, you'll find models of a wide variety of ways healthy congregations are understood and described. Some models are research-based, others denomination-based, book-based, or classified as "others." Then in chapter 3, a new relational perspective is introduced with a fresh set of signs of healthy congregations. Next, chapter 4 presents the results of a research project that tests the validity and usefulness of this original approach along with the signs of hope introduced in this chapter and signs of health introduced in chapter 2. Finally, chapter 5 considers where we go from here and offers guidelines for creating hopeful and healthy futures for congregations that emerge from the results of this study.

PRACTICAL APPLICATIONS

1. Review the biblical references in chapter 1. Then decide which one or two best anchors your understanding of Christian hope, and how they do so in your context of ministry.

2. What is an example of how there can be no hope without truth being told from your life? How about for your ministry and for your congregation's life and ministry?
3. What is an example of the way hope and faith are reciprocally related for you? How about for your ministry and for your congregation's life and ministry?
4. In what ways do you see hope helpful in facing the global challenge(s) you see as most urgent? What are several steps you and your congregation can take to face global systemic change and challenges with active hope?
5. What are some practical and creative ways the changes and challenges you are facing in your church can be connected to mission and sustained by hope?
6. Picture yourself and your youth ministry team discussing some challenges your children and youth are having to make hope happen in their lives. How can you help them set goals and find both the will and way to activate hope? How might you help family members cope with challenges and changes of aging parents soon needing memory care?
7. Consider some ways hope determines how well you live your life. How about for your congregation's life and ministry? What are some practical ways to make hope happen by choosing to hope, learning to hope, and sharing hope with others?
8. When you think about a hopeful congregation, what are one or two of the conditions in which hope seems to thrive?
9. As you reflect on the life and ministry of your congregation, for what are you most hopeful—what makes your heart sing? For what are you least hopeful—what makes your heart ache?
10. When you reflect on the way your congregation makes hope happen, how well or how poorly does it do the following: set and meet its goals? Energetically pursue its goals? Find ways to solve problems even when people get discouraged?

Note: Questions 8–10 are included in the empirical research project described in chapter 4 to test the validity and usefulness of signs of hope presented in this chapter.

FOR FURTHER STUDY

Brueggemann, Walter, ed. *Hope for the World: Mission in a Global Context.* Louisville, KY: Westminster John Knox, 2001.

———. *Truth and Hope: Essays for a Perilous Age*, edited by Louis Stulman. Louisville, KY: Westminster John Knox, 2020.

Cone, James H. *God of the Oppressed.* Rev. ed. Maryknoll, NY: Orbis, 1997.

Kwok, Pau-lan. *Postcolonial Imagination and Feminist Theology.* Louisville, KY: Westminster John Knox, 2005.

———. *Postcolonial Politics and Theology: Unraveling Empire for a Global World.* Louisville, KY: Westminster John Knox, 2021.

Lopez, Shane J. *Making Hope Happen: Create the Future You Want for Yourself and Others.* New York: Atria, 2013.

Macy, Joanna, and Chris Johnstone. *How to Face the Mess We're in with Resilience and Creative Power.* Rev. ed. Novato, CA: New World Library, 2022.

Moltmann, Jurgen. *The Spirit of Hope: Theology for a World in Peril.* Louisville, KY: Westminster John Knox, 2019.

Steinke, Peter. *A Door Set Open: Grounding Change in Mission and Hope.* Lanham, MD: Rowman & Littlefield, 2010.

World Economic Forum Global Risks. "Global Risks Perception Survey 2022–2023." https://www3.weforum.org/docs/WEF_Global_Risks_Report_2023.pdf

2

Models for Creating Healthy Congregations

IN RECENT YEARS, THERE have been myriad ways to understand and describe healthy congregations. In fact, this chapter identifies eighteen such models over the last four decades. Six are research-based, five denomination-based, five book-based, and two are classified as "others." You'll find summaries, illustrations, and comparisons of the models followed by a discussion of commonalities among these options for creating healthy congregations. Implications for our research project in chapter 4 will be noted.

RESEARCH-BASED

1. Six Themes of Alive Congregations

A study of ninety-two Presbyterian "ministering congregations" was conducted by the Vocation Agency of the United Presbyterian Church in the USA and its general director, Donald P. Smith, in the early 1980s. These churches were selected "because they demonstrated partnership in ministry between pastor and people and because their members were deeply involved in service to one another and to the community."[1] Information was sought about the activity of members in three areas of ministry: caring, justice and reconciliation, and witness and dialogue. This study discovered six recurring themes of "alive congregations" among congregations that differed widely in theological emphasis, size, geographical location, and socioeconomic context.[2]

A filmstrip, *A Tale of Three Churches*, was designed to introduce the six themes of "alive, ministering congregations." In fact, I used this approach as pastor of the Westminster United Presbyterian Church in Galena, Illinois, to help transform a "tired, apathetic" congregation into an "alive, ministering" congregation. Vision and strategy sessions with lay leaders and members of the congregation centered on these six themes leading to plans and programs that expanded the congregation's life and ministry. This process led to a pastoral-to-program church transition.[3] For example, new mission, church life, Christian formation, worship and music, planning and administration, and stewardship ministry teams were formed. As a result of these efforts, new community outreach initiatives began, educational offerings were retooled, small group and church life activities expanded, worship and music enlivened, youth and young adults empowered, new members attracted, ecumenical relations enhanced, building renovations completed, and financial stability achieved. New members included young adults, young families with children, and the newly retired.

As we'll see later, discovering grace as a way of life will reappear as one of Vibrant Christian Communities' four practices: embracing grace as a way of life. Further, we'll meet renewal among relationships again in chapter 3, along with the other three themes of alive congregations (becoming a caring community, using gifts

1. Smith, *Congregations Alive*, 13.

2. These six themes include sounding a clear call, discovering grace as a way of life, becoming a caring community, renewal through relationships, using gifts God has given, and sharing power as partners. For more information, see Smith, *Congregations Alive*, 23–24.

3. For information about this transition, see Mann, *In-Between Church*, 1998.

God has given, and sharing power as partners) among two of the 4 C's in chapter 3: community and collaboration.

2. Twelve Ways to Healthy Relationships in the Church

I have created guidelines for healthy relationships in the church derived from social science research in twelve areas.[4] More will be said about these ways to create healthy relationships in the church in chapter 3.

3. Ten Signposts for Congregational Renewal

Historian of Christianity and public theologian Diana Butler Bass identifies ten signposts or practices of renewal or transformation for congregational vitality and vibrancy, for alive, healthy, and flourishing congregations. Results of a three-year study (conducted between 2002 and 2005) of fifty moderate or liberal (centrist and progressive) churches reported in *Christianity for the Rest of Us: How the Neighborhood Church Is Transforming the Faith* identify ten signposts of congregational renewal.[5]

Most of these signposts will appear among signs of health in our research project, including welcoming strangers, listening,

---

4. These twelve areas include building relationships, leading meetings, experiencing trust, practicing forgiveness, using power, bridging cultures, practicing humility, experiencing empathy, feeling compassion, showing kindness, expressing appreciation, and doing justice. Guidelines for healthy relationships in the first six areas are found in my 2016 Rowman & Littlefield Alban publication, *Communication in the Church*, and guidelines for the remaining six areas are found in my 2021 Wipf & Stock publication, *Better Ways to Better Relationships in the Church*.

5. These ten signposts include hospitality (welcoming strangers), discernment (listening for truth), healing (entering *shalom*), contemplation (open for prayer), testimony (talking the walk), diversity (making community), justice (engaging the powers), worship (experiencing God), reflection (thinking theologically), and beauty (touching the divine.) For more information, see Bass, *Christianity*, 77–214.

making community, justice, thinking theologically, and various spiritual practices.

4. Eleven Variables for Flourishing Congregations

Canadian-based Flourishing Congregations Institute research focuses on this question: What is a flourishing congregation? Their answer, based on interviews with congregational and denominational leaders across Canadian Catholic, mainline, and conservative Protestant settings in 2016–17, is a set of eleven variables in the following three areas of congregational life and ministry: organizational ethos, inward variables, and outward variables.[6]

Based on a review of forty-six empirical congregational studies from 1972–2014, three central findings emerged from this research:[7]

- There is a divide between those who believe that flourishing entails numeric growth and those who do not.

- Depending on the Christian tradition in question, there are several partially overlapping and conflicting pictures of what constitutes a flourishing congregation, evident in the three overarching domains and several subsequent dimensions.

- Supernatural discourse figures into how leaders discuss flourishing congregations over and against secular or human-controlled narratives.

As we'll see later, these three areas of flourishing congregations (organizational ethos, internal variables, and outward variables) are similar to the Thriving Congregations Initiative's three characteristics of contextual knowledge, vibrant practices, and

---

6. These eleven variables include organizational ethos variables (self-identity, leadership, innovation, and structure and process), internal variables (diversity, hospitable community, engaged laity, and discipleship) and outward variables (evangelism, partnerships, and neighborhood involvement). For more information, see https://www.flourishingcongregations.org.

7. See Thiessen et al., "What Is a Flourishing Congregation?" See also Wong et al., *Signs of Life*.

mission clarity. Also, in the discussion at the end of this review of models, we'll see how these three parallel tracks provide a "big picture" or overarching framework into which our other models fit.

5. Six Characteristics of Spiritually Vital and Alive Congregations

Faith Communities Today is a multireligious and collaborative research initiative that has been tracking trends in the health and vitality of US religious communities since 2000. This collaborative partnership includes twenty-one denominations and religious groups. Their 2020 research project was the largest-ever congregational survey of over fifteen thousand religious communities from eighty different denominations and faith traditions. Of them, 71.3 percent were Evangelical Protestant congregations, 20.2 percent Mainline Protestant, 5.2 percent Catholic, and 1.4 percent Other Religious Traditions.[8] Spiritually vital and alive congregations are those that come together for a divine common purpose in ways that are transformative to the people within them and to their communities. The keys to creating and sustaining a vital congregation include *relationships, leadership,* and *practices.* According to the 2020 research report, about one-third of congregations surveyed reported that they are spiritually vital and alive. These congregations have six characteristics in common.[9]

---

8. According to the most recent Pew Research Center US religious landscape study, 70.6 percent are Christian, of which 25.4 percent are Evangelical Protestant, 14.7 percent are Mainline Protestant, 21.3 percent Catholic, and 0.4 percent Other Christian. See Pew Research Center, "Religious Landscape Study."

9. These characteristics include being open to incorporating new people; being willing to change to meet new challenges; having thought-provoking worship services; emphasizing religious education for both children and adults; considering it important to live out one's faith in all aspects of daily life, not just during sacred time; and having more younger people participating. For more information, see Faith Communities Today, "FACT 2020 National Survey of Congregations."

The 2020 Faith Communities Today's Twenty Years of Congregational Change report identifies concerns and challenges for flourishing, hopeful trends, and possibilities for revitalization.[10] *Concerns and challenges* for flourishing include increasing rates of decline and growing numbers of small congregations; medium-sized congregations getting smaller; and decline in member commitment and participation of large congregations. *Hopeful trends* include congregational diversity and the strength of that diversity, growing use of technology (even pre-pandemic), sustained financial health, and rising vitality and openness to change. Finally, *possibilities for revitalization* include leadership that is innovative and inspiring, a vision that is meaningful and contagious, worship that is contextual and creative, and participants that are involved and willing to change.

In the discussion at the end of this chapter, you'll find that the three keys to a vital congregation (relationships, leadership, and practices) will serve as an overarching framework into which our other models fit. Two of these three keys (leadership and practice) are among the three clusters of characteristics of thriving congregations identified by the Vibrant Faith Initiative in the next section. Also, you will find some of the six characteristics of vital congregations among the seven major areas of congregational life and ministry used to assess congregational health in the research project presented in chapter 4, including thought-provoking worship, Christian formation, and mission and outreach. Look for welcoming new people and willingness to change among recurring themes of healthy and hopeful congregations in our research results. The importance of openness to change will also be cited as a United Methodist healthy congregation practice, as a PCUSA leadership competency, as a characteristic of vital Christian communities by Brochard and Newton, and in our research project. Likewise, some hopeful trends and possibilities for revitalization will reappear in research results, including financial stability, openness to change, strong leadership, visioning, and Spirit-inspired worship.

10. See Faith Communities Today, Twenty Years of Congregational Change.

MODELS FOR CREATING HEALTHY CONGREGATIONS

6. Twenty-Three Characteristics of Thriving Congregations

Vibrant Faith's Thriving Congregations Initiative is based on fifteen congregational studies conducted between 2006 and 2020.[11] Drawn from key findings of these fifteen research studies is a vision of thriving congregations that includes twenty-three characteristics. These characteristics cluster in three primary areas: *faithful practices*, *spiritual vitality*, and *leadership*.[12]

---

11. These studies, several of which you'll recognize elsewhere in our review of models, include: Open Wide the Doors to Christ—A Study of Catholic Social Innovation for Parish Vitality (2020); Flourishing Congregations Research (2019); Seven Marks of Congregational Vitality, Presbyterian Church (USA) (2019); Vital Congregations, Faith Communities Today (2018); Congregational Vitality Project ELCA (2017); Four Essential Practices of Great Catholic Parishes (2016); What It Takes to Be a Vital Church (2016); Three Marks of Healthy Congregations (2017); Characteristics of Congregational Vitality, United Church of Christ (2015); Sixteen Drivers of Vital Congregations, United Methodist Church (2013); Forty-Four Faith Assets, Exemplary Youth Ministry Study (2010); Ten Strengths of US Congregations, Congregational Life Survey (2008); Catholic Parish Vitality Indicators, Emerging Models of Pastoral Leadership Project (2008); The Project on Congregations of Intentional Practice (2006); and Eight Quality Characteristics, Natural Church Development. For more information, see https://www.vibrantfaithprojects.org/thriving-congregations-characteristics.html.

12. Among these characteristics are *faithful practices* that guide missional congregations; that are connected, interdependent, and necessary for thriving congregations; and that require leaders to become bilingual—interpreting the biblical world into idioms of contemporary cultures. Likewise, *spiritual vitality* is strengthened when congregations do such things as have a clear identity and shared mission; adapt and innovate to meet new challenges; engage in lifelong faith formation and spiritual growth; practice discernment, hospitality, worship, theological reflection, healing, spiritual disciplines, social justice, peacemaking, and beauty; cultivate experiences of caring, safety, belonging, and acceptance; engage in outreach, service, social justice, and creation care; and use digital technologies and platforms. Further, church *leadership* characteristically has clear core values, principles, and calls to bold and risky ministry; casts a vision, mobilizes, and empowers people to achieve their goals; uses adaptive skills and innovative ways to face challenges; creates a team approach and works collaboratively; and helps people discover and utilize their gifts for ministry. (Note: A "commentary" provides descriptions of the theological and research insights behind each characteristic, and a "research summary" provides key findings from each "thriving" study.)

These characteristics of faithful practice, spiritual vitality, and leadership are similar to two of three Faith Communities Today's keys to creating and sustaining vital congregations that we just examined: practices and leadership. Spiritual vitality and leadership will also be featured as two of four signs of hopeful and healthy congregations in our research results. Moreover, as we might expect, many of these characteristics of faithful practice, spiritual vitality, and leadership are present in other models of vital, alive, flourishing, and thriving congregations. Some will also be found among practical ways the 4 C's are exemplified in chapter 3.

DENOMINATION-BASED

1. Seven Marks of Vital Congregations

Vital Congregations is a Presbyterian Church (USA) initiative of its Presbyterian Mission Agency's Theology, Formation, and Evangelism Department. Begun in 2017, here is its vision statement: "By the power of the Holy Spirit, and in authentic relationships with mid councils, we seek to equip, nurture and support church leaders to empower their congregations to renew, recover and live more fully into faithful discipleship to Jesus Christ."[13] And here is its purpose: "To work alongside leaders of existing congregations continually assessing, discerning and living into faithful actions that increase vitality through intentional spiritual practices that take them deeper into following Jesus Christ, so that their own lives are changed, congregations are transformed, and the mission of God spreads throughout particular communities and the world."[14] There are seven marks of vital congregations.[15]

---

13. See Presbyterian Church (USA), "Vital Congregations."
14. See Presbyterian Church (USA), "Vital Congregations."
15. These seven marks include lifelong discipleship, authentic evangelism, outward focus, servant leadership, Spirit-inspired worship, caring relationships, and ecclesial health. See Presbyterian Church (USA), "Immediate Toolkit," 7–12. Also, see Presbyterian Church (USA), "Vital Congregations", 8–9.

Models for Creating Healthy Congregations

One congregation began its Vital Congregations Initiative (VCI) with a church-wide Bible study and sermon series on the "Seven Marks of Congregational Vitality." Its leaders were introduced to Vital Congregations at a conference led by PCUSA national staff, trained by Presbytery facilitators, and supported through Vital Congregation cohort groups. The initial Bible study and discussions over several weeks gave people in the congregation the opportunity to share their concerns and hopes for the church. A feeling of being heard and taken seriously as a stakeholder is an especially important dimension of the vitalization process. This process helped the congregation embrace what it means to be a missional congregation. Since their participation occurred during a pastoral transition, results of a "Marks of Vitality" church-wide survey were used by the pastor-nominating committee in preparing its church mission study and a church information form used in calling a new pastor. The mission study includes a Vital Congregations Survey Report wherein 80 percent of the congregation believes it is true or very true that their church is "spiritually vital and alive"—a rating slightly higher than the 76 percent benchmark for all PCUSA congregations that have taken the survey. The culmination of the Vital Congregations Initiative for this congregation came right before their new co-pastors arrived when it held a Community Partners Sunday. Representatives of several community agencies with whom the congregation partners told their stories for the message portion of the service. It was very well received by the congregation and also served as a fresh style of worship service that demonstrated growth in their willingness to change.[16]

Many of the seven marks of vital congregations are present in other models. As we'll soon see, this similarity is especially true for four of the six United Methodist key activities of vital congregations: inviting and inspiring worship; engaged disciples in mission and outreach; gifted, empowered, and equipped lay leadership; and effective, equipped, and inspired clergy leadership. Moreover,

---

16. For another congregation's two-year VCI experience, see the Case Study of Chapel by the Sea in appendix 8.

five of these seven marks of vital congregations are included in the seven baseline signs of healthy congregations used in the research project: leadership; Spirit-inspired, thought-provoking worship; Christian formation; mission and outreach; and welcome. The other two are related to three of the 4 C's in chapter 3: caring relationships to community (ways we share with one another) and ecclesial health to both character (ways we treat one another) and collaboration (ways we work together).

2. Three Key Experiences of Congregational Vitality

As the Evangelical Lutheran Church in America (ELCA) looks ahead to the future, they "aspire to have congregations whose faith shines in their relationships with God, each other and their community. Vital congregations experience heightened worship, prayer, study of scripture, and sharing of testimony as they discern the presence and will of God in their midst."[17] In particular, vital congregations *strengthen their relationship with God, nurture relationships in the congregation,* and *have a strong presence in the community.*[18]

In 2019, a Congregational Vitality Team began using adaptive strategies to create a church-wide ELCA learning community that nurtures life-changing relationships with God, one another, and the world.[19] Its values and guiding principles include being insistent in

---

17. See North/West Lower Michigan Synod, "REVIVE."

18. *Relationship with God* is strengthened by leadership articulating how God shows up in and through the congregation; by the congregation having a clear understanding of God's larger mission and members knowing their purpose in their time and place; and by the congregation articulating that purpose and creating a plan for implementation. *Relationships are nurtured* among pastor(s) and staff and as members create a loving community with good communication, as people work together respectfully, and as there is a sense of ownership and belonging that drives the commitment and engagement in the mission of the church. Finally, *strong presence in the community* occurs by welcoming the stranger, sharing Christ's love, and partnering to make a positive impact in the community.

19. See Evangelical Lutheran Church of America, https://blogs.elca.org/congregationalvitality/meet-the-elca-congregational-vitality-team.

collaboration, supportive of innovation and creativity, intentionally inclusive and anti-racist, radically relational, committed to learning multiplication, and ardent about leadership development.[20]

These three key experiences—our relationships with God, one another, and the world—will prove to be a unifying theme among our eighteen conceptions of healthy congregations in this chapter. We'll also see these three experiences in UCC's framework of connecting to God, one another, and the world, and in Thriving Congregations Initiative's emphasis on our relationship with God, connecting with each other, and our contribution to the world. Finally, chapter 3 will center on one of these key experiences: our relationships with one another.

3. Six Key Activities of Vital Congregations

This is the United Methodist Church's version of "vital congregations" with its call to be Spirit-filled, forward-leaning communities of believers that welcome all people, make disciples of Jesus Christ, and serve like Christ through justice and mercy ministries.[21] Vital congregations have six key activities.[22]

This initiative grew out of a Vital Congregations Research Project completed in 2010 that found four key drivers of congregational vitality: pastoral leadership, multiple small groups, diverse worship styles, and a high percentage of spiritually engaged laity in leadership roles. Key strategies for creating vital congregations were also developed.[23]

---

20. See Evangelical Lutheran Church of America, https://blogs.elca.org/congregationalvitality/meet-the-elca-congregational-vitality-team.

21. See United Methodist Church, "UMC Vital Congregations Planning Guide," http://s3.amazonaws.com/Website_Properties/how-we-serve/documents/vital-congregation-planning-guide.pdf.

22. These six characteristics include inviting and inspiring worship; engaged disciples in mission and outreach; gifted, empowered, and equipped lay leadership; effective, equipped, and inspired clergy leadership; small group ministries; and strong children's and youth ministries.

23. For more information, see United Methodist Church, "UMC Call to Action."

Signs of Hope and Health in Mainline Churches

Based on the findings of this study, a "Call to Action" invited all United Methodist churches to make congregational vitality the church's "true first priority" for at least a decade.[24] A planning guide was created for use by congregations to carry out this Call to Action and the six key activities and sixteen key strategies of a vital congregation.[25]

Here's an example that illustrates how this action is being carried out. The Michigan Conference of the United Methodist Church's "Healthy Congregations" website poses and reflects on this question: "What is a healthy congregation? Have you wondered what needs to happen to develop a church that knows how to manage the changing landscapes of 'what it means to be a church' today? Today, more than ever, churches are asking that question. It seems as if some churches are managing those changing demands seamlessly and others are struggling and divided. What's [sic] makes one work and the other not? The answer lies in how those churches are managing change, communication, differences of opinions, conflict, and resources."[26] And that's not all. The website goes on to identify practices of healthy congregations.[27] Moreover, workshops on creating healthy congregations are offered by the conference with trained facilitators.

These United Methodist key activities of vital congregations are similar to the PCUSA marks of vital congregations, including engaged discipleship, lifelong learning, authentic evangelism, outward focus, empowered leadership, and inspired worship. Likewise, several practices are among the 4 C's approach introduced in chapter 3, including ways people create community, communicate, treat each other, and work together. Managing change is

---

24. For more information, see United Methodist Church, "Bishops Support Church Reforms, Accountability."

25. For more information, see United Methodist Church, "UMC Vital Congregations Planning Guide."

26. See Michigan Conference, "Healthy Congregations."

27. These practices include systems thinking; acceptance of differences; focus on strengths; focus on mission/vision; management of anxiety; conflict and change; flexible and creative thinking; intentional leadership development; and spiritual care.

present in other models, while systems thinking, acceptance of differences, and managing anxiety will reappear in Steinke's principles of health, as well as in Brubaker's gates of healthy restorative churches.

4. Ten Factors of Congregational Vitality

Ministerial leadership matters, and it profoundly impacts the vitality of congregations. So concludes a 2015 United Church of Christ "Congregational Vitality and Ministerial Excellence" research report.[28] Overall, UCC congregations think highly of their pastor's qualities, skills, and abilities. Likewise, most consider their churches to be spiritually vital places that help people connect to God, one another, and the world.[29] This report goes on to identify ministerial leadership skills that correlate with congregational vitality factors. In fact, four leadership skills are identified.[30] Ten factors of congregational vitality are also identified.[31]

It is important to note that the UCC's threefold pattern—connection to God, one another, and the world—parallels both ELCA's three keys experiences of congregational vitality already cited (relationships with God, each other, and their community) and the Thriving Congregations three emphases we'll discover later on: our relationship with God, connecting with each other,

---

28. See United Church of Christ, "Congregational Vitality and Ministerial Excellence," 4.

29. This research report credits this definition of congregational vitality to ELCA researcher Linda Bobbitt in "Measuring Congregational Vitality," 467–84.

30. These leadership skills include communicating appropriately, taking initiative in leadership, framing and testing a vision in community, and equipping and motivating. See United Church of Christ, "Congregational Vitality and Ministerial Excellence," 37.

31. These factors include excitement about the future; clear sense of mission; meaningful activities; readiness to try something new; incorporating newcomers into congregational life; seeking out and using gifts of members of all ages; building strong, healthy relationships among members; managing disagreements in a healthy, respectful manner; equipping members to share their faith with others; and interacting with the local community. See United Church of Christ, "Congregational Vitality and Ministerial Excellence," 35.

and our contribution to the world. Then, as we'll see in the discussion at the end of this chapter, this threefold pattern will become a unifying theme into which other models will fit. Likewise, the leadership skills of communication, visioning, and equipping will reappear among the 4 C's in chapter 3. Moreover, while also present in several other models, we'll revisit vitality factors relating to a clear sense of mission, trying something new, incorporating newcomers, using members' gifts, healthy relationships, managing disagreements, sharing faith, and community interaction in the research results of chapter 4.

5. *Thirty-Three Leadership Competencies*

The Church Leadership Connection is a Presbyterian Church (USA) internet-based matching and referral system.[32] It uses thirty-three "leadership competencies" to match pastors and congregations in these four areas: theological/spiritual interpreter, communication, organizational leadership, and interpersonal engagement.[33]

More will be said about these leadership competencies in chapter 3 regarding how people work with one another in the church.

---

32. See Office of the General Assembly, "Church Leadership Connection.".

33. Competencies in these four areas include: *theological/spiritual interpreter* (compassionate, preaching and worship leadership, lifelong learner, hopeful, spiritual maturity, and teacher); *communication* (communicator, public communicator, technologically savvy, bilingual, and media communicator); *organizational leadership* (advisor, contextualization, externally aware, risk taker, willingness to engage conflict, organizational agility, financial manager, collaboration, change agent, culturally proficient, entrepreneurial, task manager, decision making, strategy and vision, and funds developer); and *interpersonal engagement* (interpersonal engagement, motivator, initiative, self-differentiation, bridge builder, personal resilience, and flexibility). (Note: This matching system has been used for the last fifteen years and is currently being revised using a new competency survey. See Office of the General Assembly, "Understanding the CLC Competency Survey.")

Models for Creating Healthy Congregations

BOOK-BASED

1. Four Practices of Vibrant Christian Communities

Professor of Church in Society Christine D. Pohl identifies four specific Christian practices to build and sustain vibrant communities in her book *Living into Community: Cultivating Practices That Sustain Us.*[34]

Embracing grace as a way of life is also one of Congregations Alive's six themes. Practicing hospitality is also one of the spiritual vitality practices of the Thriving Congregations and one of the ten signposts of Congregational Renewal. Making and keeping promises and living truthfully are unique to Pohl's practices.

2. Ten Principles of Healthy Congregations

Peter Steinke's 1996 Alban publication, *Healthy Congregations: A Systems Approach*, identifies ten "principles of health."[35] It views health as wholeness with a dynamic balance with the body's chemistry and the functioning of its various parts. Here is the way Steinke explains this balance in relationship to organizations

---

34. These four practices include embracing grace as a way of life, making and keeping promises, living truthfully, and practicing hospitality. For more information about these practices, see Pohl, *Living into Community*.

35. These ten principles include the following: Wholeness is not attainable (but it can be approximated); illness is the necessary complement to health (it is all right to be sick, feel burdened, and be down); the body has innate healing abilities (no one can give you—or the congregation—what you don't already have); agents of disease are not causes of disease (all disease processes are enabled); all illness is biopsychosocial (wow! everything is connected); the subtle precedes the gross (early detection is the best treatment); everybody is different (there's no universal treatment for every organism—or congregation); a healthy circulatory system is the keystone of health and healing (feedback systems promote health); breathing properly is nourishing to the whole body (the Spirit must be active among the members of the body of Christ); and the brain is the largest secreting organ of the body, the health maintenance organization (HMO) of the body (the mind converts ideas into biochemical realities). For more information about these principles, see Steinke, *Healthy Congregations*, 15.

like the church: "Like an organism, an organization must adapt to disturbances and challenges to its balance. Both organisms and organizations are more apt to become sick after major losses, disruptive events, and prominent changes. All put stress on a system's balance. Congregations seek wholeness."[36]

Interestingly, in the preface to the 2006 edition, Steinke says if he were to make any changes in the original manuscript today, he would place more emphasis on the key role of "mood, tone, and spirit" in enhancing congregational health. Then he goes on to make this further comment: "I wonder if the 'mood, tone, and spirit' of a congregation isn't closely related to having a clear purpose, which in healthy congregations is focus on mission. When life is meaningful, people have more energy and hope. The philosopher Fredrick Nietzche said that if Christians wanted others to believe in their Redeemer, they needed to look more redeemed."[37] Steinke develops this emphasis in his 2010 Alban publication *A Door Set Open: Grounding Change in Mission and Hope*. As we noticed in chapter 1, this connection between mission and hope is an important one.

Steinke is not unique in comparing healthy organisms with healthy congregations. Later, we'll see that Brubaker's "restorative congregations" approach also compares congregational health to a healthy human body. Also, several other models feature systems thinking, as we saw in the United Methodist Michigan Conference's practices of healthy congregations, and as we will see in Rowe's features of thriving Christian communities and in Brubaker's gates of healthy restorative churches.

3. Twelve Characteristics of Healthy Congregations

In their recent book *Vital Christian Community: Twelve Characteristics of Healthy Congregations*, Episcopalian priests and consultants Phil Brochard and Alissa Newton identify twelve characteristics

---

36. Steinke, *Healthy Congregations*, 16.
37. Steinke, *Healthy Congregations*, 2nd ed., ix–x.

of healthy congregations to help congregations grow in health, faithfulness, and effectiveness.[38] Models are introduced for each characteristic as tools congregational leaders can use to develop that characteristic in their context. Especially helpful are retreat designs for leadership bodies featuring such topics as Christian community, faith development, and the Benedictine life.

The first characteristic, creating a sense of purpose, is related to setting and meeting goals as a way to make hope happen, as noted in chapter 1. Having a healthy emotional culture is related to some of Steinke's principles of health. And then several characteristics are related to recurring themes of hope and health that will be identified in our research project, including change, focus, leadership, and spiritual practices. Moreover, several characteristic will reappear among our 4 C's in chapter 3, including experiencing trust, building relationships, and bridging cultures as ways to create community; engaging conflict and exercising curiosity as ways to communicate; and visioning, discerning, partnering, and engaging gifts as ways to collaborate. Finally, several characteristics are found among the PCUSA leadership competencies, including self-differentiation, willingness to engage conflict, cultural proficiency, ability to lead change, strategizing and visioning, and being a bridge builder.

4. Seven Key Practices for Healthy Congregations

Episcopal priest and church consultant Tom Ehrich observes that many congregations face similar challenges and identifies seven key factors that determine a church's health in his book *Church Wellness: A Best Practices Guide to Nurturing Healthy Congregations*.[39]

---

38. In these twelve characteristics, healthy congregations articulate a sense of purpose; are reliably transformative; ground themselves in practice; practice trust; are curious; respond to context and people; reflect on their lives together; are open to change; are collaborative; engage in productive conflict; have a healthy emotional culture; and lead with differentiation. See Brochard and Newton, *Vital Christian Community*, xiv.

39. These seven factors include developing members, nurturing leaders, communicating effectively, growing spiritually, welcoming young adults,

He then offers guidance on steps to nurture a faith community: best practices for doing the work of the church that lead to health and effectiveness.

Whereas Ehrich's best practices arise out of his research and consulting, his factors of communication, spiritual life, welcoming, and listening are addressed in many of our other models and will be presented among findings from our research project. Less common among our models is his guidance for evaluating the effectiveness of a congregation's programs.

5. Six Features of Thriving Christian Communities

Duke Divinity School's C. Kavin Rowe identifies six specific features of the early Christian communities from the Acts of the Apostles in his book *Leading Christian Communities*.[40] In this collection of essays, Rowe illustrates these six patterns with stories of communities that are shaping Christian leaders for the flourishing of their congregations in a disconnected culture. While other models address an understanding of community, engaging disagreements, cultural resilience, networking, and listening, these essays offer unique focus on visibility, provision for the weak, suffering, humor, and power. Rowe also uniquely derives his features from the New Testament.

---

listening to parishioners' needs, and taking stock of programs. For further information, see Ehrich, *Church Wellness*.

40. These six features include networking, visibility, making room for the weak, incorporating disagreements, why community exists, and suffering. He also addresses the topics of humor as a mark of life-giving leadership, cultural resilience, listening, and power. For more information, see Rowe, *Leading Christian Communities*.

OTHERS

1. Three Characteristics of Thriving Congregations

In 2019, Lilly Endowment launched its Thriving Congregations Initiative that "aims to help congregations strengthen their ministries so they can better help people deepen their relationships with God, enhance their connections with each other, and contribute to the flourishing of their communities and the world."[41] Lilly's initiative asks the question, "What makes congregations flourish?" They answer that local congregations are the primary form of Christian community, and those that thrive share three characteristics:[42] *contextual knowledge* (relational and relevant ministries emerge from understanding rapidly changing communities), *mission clarity* (a strong sense of identity and values draws from a church's theological and ecclesial tradition), and *vibrant practices* (common rituals help congregations effectively address new challenges and nurture spirituality vitality).

A 100-member congregation describes their Thriving Congregation Initiative participation this way: "We are part of a Presbytery-wide initiative to become a 'Learning Congregation.' The 'church' has changed dramatically in its position in society. Churches are needing to change their understanding of their role in their community. This spiritual practice of 'listening to your community' helps them thrive as viable partners in God's activity all around them. In turn, it helps communities grasp the importance of the church's role among them. Our thriving congregations ministry team will be coming to you for input and with participatory learning opportunities as we proceed."[43] Among these learning opportunities are a listening-skill-building seminar, a panel discussion by members of transgender neighbors, and presentations by the directors of a new neighborhood career exploration and skill development program for multiracial youth ages fourteen to

---

41. See https://thrivingcongregations.org.

42. See https://thrivingcongregations.org.

43. I am grateful to Rainier Beach Presbyterian Church, Seattle, Washington, for this description.

twenty-four now partnering with the congregation. Several grants have added well-received creative and innovative dimensions to the congregation's worship and music. These learning and imaginative activities are attracting Gen Z and millennial young adults and families who are eagerly becoming involved in the congregation's life and ministry. Here are comments from these new members:

- "We love the jamming at the end of each service."
- "We were particularly interested in finding a LGBTQ+ affirming church."
- "I like the focus on refugees and migrants."
- "I felt included and loved."
- "I am excited about the Thriving Congregations Initiative work and want to be part of it."

As noted earlier, these three Thriving Congregations Initiative characteristics (contextual knowledge, mission clarity, and vibrant practices) are similar to the three Flourishing Congregations Institute areas of congregational life and ministry (organizational ethos, internal variables, and inward variables). Also, as noted earlier, the aims of deepening relationships with God, enhancing connections with each other, and contributing to the world are similar to both the ELCA's key experiences of our relationships with God, with one another, and with the world, and to UCC's model of connecting to God, one another, and the world. In the discussion section at the end of our review of models, we'll see how this threefold pattern of compatible aims, key experiences, and connecting provides an overarching framework into which our other models will fit.

2. Three Marks of Healthy Congregations

This "healthy congregations" approach comes from the Restorative Church project begun in 2016.[44] It draws on work by Mennonite

---

44. For information on this project, see Restorative Church, "Healthy

Models for Creating Healthy Congregations

Professor of Organizational Studies David Brubaker and his three marks of healthy congregations.[45] This approach suggests that a healthy inside dynamic can openly engage with everything outside by focusing on twelve "gates" of a healthy restorative church.[46]

This important note of clarification needs to be made about these "gates": "This listing pertains to the relational corporate health of a church body and not to every aspect of church life and mission. Clearly a healthy church tends to other matters as well, including worship, outreach, leadership, etc. A healthy church is also attuned to racial reconciliation and responsive to all injustices. Since love is the hallmark of Christian identity as described in the New Testament, the relational health of church members is viewed as being foundational to all other areas of church life and mission. Ultimately, a church's outreach is as strong as its inreach."[47]

The outward and inward dynamics of this approach are similar to the Flourishing Congregations Institute's three areas of flourishing congregations: organizational ethos, internal variables, and outward variables. Additionally, the comparison of a congregation's health to a healthy human body is reminiscent of Steinke's likeness between healthy organisms and healthy organizations, as this statement from Ted Lewis illustrates: "To keep a body healthy, you have to feed it well, maintain exercise, minimize stress, and get plenty of rest! If it gets sick, don't just treat the symptoms."[48] Moreover, the focus on relational health is similar to the 4 C's emphasis on relational health in chapter 3.

Congregations."

45. These three marks include a clear and shared center; clear but permeable boundaries; and focus outward, not just inward. See Brubaker, "Three Marks of Healthy Congregations."

46. These gates include forgiveness, interpersonal reconciliation, conversation, self-differentiation, disagreements, anxieties, healing, acts of love, listening and speech, peacemaking, religious education, and outside facilitation. See Restorative Church, "Healthy Congregations."

47. Restorative Church, "Healthy Congregations."

48. Restorative Church, "Healthy Congregations."

DISCUSSION

Two of the research-based conceptions of healthy congregations lead us to "big picture" or overarching perspectives. First, the Faith Communities Today 2020 research project's survey of over fifteen thousand religious communities from eighty denominational and faith traditions discovered these three overarching keys to creating and sustaining vital congregations:

- Relationships
- Leadership
- Practices

Likewise, as noted earlier, two of these three keys (leadership and practice) are among the three clusters of characteristics of thriving congregations identified by the Vibrant Faith Initiative based on fifteen congregational research studies (eight of which are among our eighteen models).

Second, the Flourishing Congregations Institute's research based on interviews with congregations and denominational leaders across Catholic, mainline, and conservative Protestant settings discovered these three overarching areas of flourishing congregational life and ministry:

- Organizational ethos variables
- Internal variables
- Outward variables

Also, as noted earlier, the three Thriving Congregations Initiative characteristics also follow this pattern:[49]

- Contextual knowledge
- Vibrant practices
- Mission clarity

49. Organizational ethos and contextual knowledge are related in that both center in context—organizational context and community context, respectively.

Most or all the other fourteen conceptions fit fairly well in one or both overarching perspectives. Whether healthy congregations are described in terms of themes, ways, signposts, characteristics, marks, experience, activities, factors, competencies, practices, principles, or features, most of these varying descriptions may be located among relationships, leadership, and practices, and/or among the threefold organizational/contextual, internal/practices, and outward/mission integrating pattern.

Another unifying theme among the eighteen conceptions of healthy congregations in this chapter is to think in terms of the ELCA's three key experiences of our relationships with God, one another, and the world; with UCC's model of connecting to God, one another, and the world; and with Thriving Congregation's aims of deepening relationships with God, connecting with each another, and contributing to the world. In the next chapter, chapter 3, we'll consider a relational perspective in our quest for signs of healthy congregations. In chapter 3, it will be our relationships with one another in the church on which we'll focus.

Then in chapter 4, a research project will test several hypotheses about healthy congregations, including one drawn from these eighteen conceptions. Specifically, baseline questions will be created to identify signs of a healthy congregation, to assess congregational health, and to assess how well healthy congregations do in these seven major areas of their life and ministry: leadership; biblical and theological anchoring; Christian formation; worship; mission and outreach; welcome; and finances.

Finally, in chapter 5, we'll consider guidelines for creating hopeful and healthy futures for mainline churches that emerge from the results of this study.

PRACTICAL APPLICATIONS

1. Which of the eighteen ways of understanding and describing healthy congregations strike you as most accurate and useful? What features do they most have in common?

2. Many church leaders and members would like their congregations to be vital, lively, thriving, or flourishing. What do you see as one or two signs of a healthy congregation?
3. From "very poor" to "excellent," how do you rate the overall health of your congregation?
4. How about the overall effectiveness of leaders in your congregation?
5. How about the way your congregation anchors its life and ministry biblically and theologically?
6. How about providing Spirit-inspired, thought-provoking worship?
7. How about providing Christian formation?
8. How about engaging in mission and outreach activities?
9. How about welcoming new people?
10. How about achieving financial stability?

Note: Questions 2–10 are included in the empirical research project described in chapter 4 to test the validity and usefulness of signs of healthy congregations presented in this chapter.

FOR FURTHER STUDY

Bass, Diana Butler. *Christianity for the Rest of Us: How the Neighborhood Church Is Transforming the Faith.* New York: HarperCollins, 2006.

Brochard, Phil and Alissabeth Newton. *Vital Christian Community: Twelve Characteristics of Healthy Congregations.* New York: Church Publishing, 2022.

Ehrich, Tom. *Church Wellness: A Best Practices Guide to Nurturing Healthy Congregations.* New York: Church Publishing, 2008.

Evangelical Lutheran Church of America. "Congregational Vitality: Stories and Learning." https://blogs.elca.org/congregationalvitality/meet-the-elca-congregational-vitality-team.

Faith Communities Today. "FACTs on Spiritually Vital Congregations: FACT 2020 National Survey of Congregations." https://www.hartfordinternational.edu/sites/default/files/2022-09/FACTs-on-Spiritually-Vital-Congregations-Report_Sep-2022%20%281%29.pdf.

Faith Communities Today. "Twenty Years of Congregational Change: The 2020 Faith Communities Today Overview." https://faithcommunitiestoday.org/wp-content/uploads/2021/10/Faith-Communities-Today-2020-Summary-Report.pdf.

Flourishing Congregations Institute. https://www.flourishingcongregations.org.

Lilly Endowment. https://thrivingcongregations.org.

Presbyterian Church (USA). "Vital Congregations." https://www.presbyterianmission.org/ministries/theology-%20formation-and-evangelism/vital-congregations.

Rowe, C. Kavin. *Leading Christian Communities*. Grand Rapids: Eerdmans, 2023.

Steinke, Peter L. *Healthy Congregations: A Systems Approach*. 2nd ed. Herndon, VA: Alban Institute, 2006.

Vibrant Faith Thriving Congregations Initiative. "Thriving Congregations Characteristics." https://www.vibrantfaithprojects.org/thriving-congregations-characteristics.html.

United Church of Christ. "Congregational Vitality and Ministerial Excellence: Intersections and Possibilities for Ministry." https://new.uccfiles.com/pdf/UCC-Congregational-Vitality-and-Ministerial-Excellence-Report.pdf.

United Methodist Church. "UMC Vital Congregations Planning Guide." http://s3.amazonaws.com/Website_Properties/how-we-serve/documents/vital-congregation-planning-guide.pdf.

3

Signs of Healthy Congregations
A 4 C's Relational Perspective

What does the LORD *require of you but to do justice, and to love kindness, and to walk humbly with your God?*
—MICAH 6:8

You shall love the Lord your God with all your heart, and with all your soul, and with all your strength, and with all you mind; and your neighbor as yourself.
—LUKE 10:27

By this everyone will know that you are my disciples, if you have love for one another.
—JOHN 13:35

Now as an elder myself and a witness of the sufferings of Christ, as well as one who shares in the glory to be revealed, I exhort the elders among you to tend the flock of God that is in your charge, exercising the oversight, not under compulsion but willingly, as God would have you do it—not for sordid gain but eagerly. Do not lord it over those in your charge, but be examples to the flock. And when the chief shepherd appears, you will win the crown of glory that never fades away.

—1 Peter 5:1–4

It's all about relationships!

It should not be surprising that Christian life and ministry is centered in relationships. In fact, the core of our faith—Jesus's two great commandments—is centered in loving God, ourselves, and our neighbors. Moreover, we find the centrality of our relationship with one another in the church from Jesus's words in John 13:35: "By this everyone will know that you are my disciples, if you have love for one another." This centers our faith and lives in our relationships with God, with ourselves, with one another, and with the world. Neither should it surprise that the literature reviewed in chapter 2 reveals a unifying theme among the eighteen diverse conceptions of healthy congregations: our relationships with God, with one another, and with the world.

It is our relationships with one another in the church on which we'll focus our attention in this chapter. From a relational perspective, where do you see signs of health in the church? In what areas of the church's life and ministry might we search for signs of health? When I think of places to look, or search for words or concepts that best capture or anchor signs of health in the church, this 4 "C's" framework comes to mind:

- Community
- Communication
- Character
- Collaboration

Community has to do with *ways we share with one another*, communication with *ways we interact with one another*, character with *ways we treat one another*, and collaboration with *ways we work with one another*.

Signs of Hope and Health in Mainline Churches

Before turning to each of these relational signs of healthy congregations, however, it is important to keep in mind what makes our relationships with one another meaningful, satisfying, or fulfilling in the first place. There are four foundational or underlying qualities of relational health: openness, acceptance, growth, and warmth. Openness leads to the freedom and safety to share those things in our personal lives that matter most. Acceptance means that what we share is treated with respect, nonjudgmentally, and reverently as on holy ground. Warmth refers to qualities or feelings of intimacy, appreciation, and affection. Finally, growth is fostered through a curiosity that sparks a desire to learn and through the support and empowerment necessary for actualizing our God-given human potential.

Elsewhere I've introduced the following guidelines for relational health and satisfaction:[1]

- Guidelines for openness: sharing, risking, and assertiveness
- Guidelines for acceptance: listening, trusting, and empathy
- Guidelines for growth: supporting, empowering, and curiosity
- Guidelines for warmth: caring, connecting, and mutuality

As we turn now to our 4 C's perspective for signs of healthy congregations, we'll find traces of these guidelines for relational health and satisfaction. Here then are signs of healthy congregations, including a synopsis of practical ways each is exemplified drawn from the latest relational and social science empirical research.

Community: Ways We Share with One Another

Imagine that it's time for your monthly sharing and support group to begin. With coffee in hand and chitchat wrapping up, group members share their overall wellbeing from 1 to 10. You've had

---

1. See Kirkpatrick, *Communication in the Church*, 122.

an especially challenging last several weeks and are invited to begin sharing since you had the lowest number. Group members have developed a deep level of trust with one another from the careful listening and nonjudgmental climate you experience. You can count on talking about those things in your life that matter most because of the openness, acceptance, and warmth you find in the group. Each time you meet, you get to share what makes your heart both sing and ache, knowing that you will receive the care, encouragement, and support that keeps you going, helps you grow, and sustains your wellbeing. These qualities of healthy small group life create a safe atmosphere for intimate sharing and give you courage to share what's been happening in your life since you last met.

This small group has created a sense of community through members sharing and supporting one another. Christian community grows out of the biblical concept of *koinonia*: "to share with someone in something."[2] It is a relational term and can be best described as *close personal relationships*. It has to do with building relationships with one another and belonging to one another. A sense of community requires a type of interpersonal intimacy and communication characterized by our four relational qualities of openness, acceptance, growth, and warmth.

Other signs or ways we share with one another and create healthy Christian community include:

- Building relationships
- Affirming and supporting
- Experiencing trust
- Showing empathy
- Practicing forgiveness
- Bridging cultures

Building relationships includes such behaviors as perception checking; creating meaning; using both verbal and nonverbal

---

2. See Kittel, *Theological Dictionary of the New Testament*, 804.

communication; diminishing defensiveness and fostering a supportive climate; raising your listening IQ; and facing and handling conflict.[3] Rather than unconsciously assume we understand one another, it pays to check our perceptions by paraphrasing one another's meanings, especially when our conversations include strongly held ideas or below-the-surface feelings. Pausing and taking the time to check our perception of what each of us is getting at may be the single most important skill we can use to help us build healthy relationships. Creating meaning is essential in understanding one another, as I've commented elsewhere: "The communication process is more complex than either shooting our ideas to someone or batting ideas back and forth. So, it pays to be careful and approach communication as a dynamic, meaning-centered transaction in which a relationship emerges between people."[4] Using both verbal and nonverbal communication also helps us understand the meaning of our words by engaging our facial expressions and varying our tone of voice. While integral to building relationships, communication climates, effective listening, and handling conflict will be covered separately in topics to follow.

Affirming and supporting features Paul's urging in 1 Thess 5:11 to "encourage one another and build one another up." It includes offering positive feedback and expressing mutual care for one another. Many of us haven't received a lot of affirmative messages, especially in our formative years—at least in comparison to the plethora of negative feedback and disconfirming messages we encounter. Consequently, many of us have a lower view of ourselves than is accurate. One way to increase our capacity and skill of affirming one another is to remember to let people know when you appreciate something they've done or said. Another way to raise our view of ourselves to a more accurate level is to consider using the group activity called "The Strength Bombardment Exercise."[5]

---

3. For more information about these behaviors, see Kirkpatrick, *Communication in the Church*, 1–31.

4. Kirkpatrick, *Communication in the Church*, 4.

5. See Kirkpatrick, *Communication in the Church*, appendix C, for an explanation of this activity and how to use it.

It was consistently the most valuable experience for students in my interpersonal communication classes during my college and seminary teaching career. Then, too, we can learn to diminish defensiveness and foster a supportive climate as mentioned previously in building relationships. We can learn to use description rather than evaluation, problem orientation rather than control, spontaneity rather than strategy, empathy rather than neutrality, equality rather than superiority, and provisionalism rather than certainty.[6] These six sets of supportive and defensive climates from research by communication scholar Jack Gibb remain the single most useful insight I've discovered in all my years of study, teaching, and research in the field of interpersonal and small-group communication.

The *experience of trust* means being able to rely on someone. It involves linking risk and trust by mutual vulnerability, sufficient information, and ethical conduct. Good intentions and competency are required. Healthy relationships are created by successfully navigating the risks and uncertainties associated with suspicion and reliance. Trust is also often strained or broken during times of disagreement in our conversations, discussions, and decision-making. There is considerable variation in the time it takes to heal, repair, and restore broken relations and a variety of ways to find common ground. Trust produces an openness, acceptance, warmth, and support in our communication that creates healthier relationships.[7]

Showing empathy is a multifaceted process of sharing, understanding, and responding to others' experiences. As British Pakistani author Mohsin Hamid puts it, "Empathy is about finding echoes of another person in yourself." It is what the apostle Paul urges in Rom 12:15: "Rejoice with those who rejoice, weep with those who weep." Empathy plays a valuable role in the caring

---

6. See Gibb, "Defensive Communication," 141–48. For more information about these supportive and defensive climates, see Kirkpatrick, *Communication in the Church*, 5–8.

7. For more information about experiencing trust, see Kirkpatrick, *Communication in the Church*, 55–80.

process; in moral development, judgment, motivation, and responsibility; in the arts; and in society. Gender and intercultural differences affect our giving and receiving empathy. Empathy also fosters careful communication and creates healthier relationships.[8]

The *practice of forgiveness* is a complex journey that people experience in diverse ways and time frames, depending on previous experience and role models. It is neither inherently good nor bad, so we must learn when to grant forgiveness, to withhold forgiveness, and to reduce unforgiveness if we are to move forward from broken relationships toward healing and repair. Forgiveness is a gift—soft on sin without being permissive or condoning wrongful behavior. Grace is required so that we neither overlook sin nor sidestep justice. Forgiveness, though, doesn't always mean forgetting. Sometimes hurt is deep and healing long-term. We may need to forgive and move forward so as not to permit ourselves to get stuck or allow painful memories to haunt us. A forgiving spirit leads us to be patient with ourselves, others, and God, and often requires attentive listening and sensible handling of conflict. It joins truth and justice to create peace—depending on what victims need or want from their offenders.[9]

Bridging cultures includes paying attention to ways cultural differences affect how we communicate and build healthy relationships. For example, eye contact, tone of voice, how we regulate time, and how we express emotions all vary between cultures. How we use silence, touch, personal space, and gestures also vary culturally. Cultural factors affect our understanding and practice of forgiveness. We must learn to be flexible intercultural communicators by managing cultural differences adaptively and creatively in a wide variety of situations. Cultural sensitivity leads to more inclusive group participation and decision-making in a multicultural community. Power differences affect multicultural communication,

---

8. For more information about showing empathy, see Kirkpatrick, *Better Ways*, 19–45.

9. For more information about these guidelines for practicing forgiveness, see Kirkpatrick, *Communication in the Church*, 82–115.

how we relate to difference, and how we overcome reluctance to welcome diversity.[10]

Communication: Ways We Interact with One Another

As my mainline pastor colleagues gathered for our weekly lectionary text study, one of our ELCA colleagues released her lingering frustration from last night's parish council meeting: "The biggest problem in my church is communication breakdowns," to which my PCUSA, UCC, UMC, and other ELCA colleagues replied one after the other, "Me too," "Me too," "Me too," and "Me too."

Healthy interpersonal, small-group, and organizational communication are central subjects in my speech communication academic discipline, and relationship science research has finally taken its place among the social sciences. In fact, I've become aware in recent years that handbooks of research are now published on such topics as building relationships, leading meetings, experiencing trust, practicing forgiveness, feeling compassion, and bridging cultures—topics at the heart of avoiding communication breakdowns and fostering healthy relational communication.

Here, then, are ways we interact with one another that are signs of healthy communication:

- Engaging conflict
- Listening attentively
- Finding common ground
- Technological savvy
- Expressing appreciation
- Exercising curiosity

When we consider *engaging conflict*, we'd do well to take seriously the apostle Paul's appeal to Christians at Corinth to be agreeable and not to allow dissension to emerge. He says, "Be

---

10. For more information about bridging cultures, see Kirkpatrick, *Communication in the Church*, 9–10.

united in the same mind and the same purpose" (1 Cor 1:10). In other words, rather than allow attitudinal division, quarreling, or interpersonal bickering to take root, Paul says to *keep it together*. There are no magical pathways to pain-free conflict. However, we can help people be more careful in how they handle their differences by paying attention to facing conflict, ways to view conflict, ways to handle conflict, identifying and describing feelings, and problem solving.[11]

For example, during times of conflict caused by the clash of strong differences of opinion, I've discovered a three-question *modus operandi* for engaging conflict. This conflict-management process provides the clarity and direction needed to move from uproar to thriving—from being stuck to finding a solution. First, what are we differing about? This question identifies the primary issue about which people differ and gives focus to the conflict-management process. Second, what do we each want? This question clarifies each of our goals and provides the parameters for a satisfactory outcome. Third, what other options do we have? This question gives direction for finding a satisfactory solution. It moves us from getting stuck in an anxious, spiraling, out-of-control, either-or mentality to a calm, orderly, engaging search for creative alternatives that are acceptable to everyone—mutually agreeable alternatives that address the issue and satisfy everyone's goals. I find that as much as 80 percent of the time, a 100 percent satisfactory, mutually acceptable path to *getting it together* is available if we'll just pause, then calmly and courageously take the time to engage conflict by asking and using these three questions.

Listening attentively adopts this helpful perspective from Jas 1:19: "Let everyone be quick to listen, [and] slow to speak." Jesus also gives preferential treatment to listening. For example, in the four Gospels, while Jesus is asked nearly two hundred questions, he answers fewer than ten. Sometimes he answers questions indirectly, sometimes he remains silent, and sometimes he answers a question by asking another question. Jesus prefers to ask questions

---

11. For more information about these five ways to engage conflict, see Kirkpatrick, *Communication in the Church*, 20–27.

rather than to provide answers. He asks more than three hundred questions, far more than he is asked. Questions function to invite and facilitate discussion, gain information, inspire learning, challenge opposing views, prompt reactions, stimulate thinking, reveal motivation, precipitate action, disarm defensiveness, and build closeness. Most adults spend the majority of our waking hours communicating, and of this time, listening accounts for nearly half. Unfortunately, we spend a lot of time doing something at which many of us are not very adept. Fortunately, we can learn to acquire the knowledge and skills to improve our listening behavior—to raise our listening IQ. Improving our listening behavior includes paying attention to listening facts and fallacies, listening benefits, listening styles, listening goals, listening processes, and listening power.[12]

Finding common ground keeps us from getting locked into "either-or," "I'm-right-you're-wrong" accusations rather than finding "both-and" pathways. We get stuck and lack direction in our search to find a path through conflict that leaves trust intact. Sometimes, we must settle for compromise during times of disagreement and decision-making. However, as mentioned earlier about managing conflict, I have discovered that as much as 80 percent of the time, a 100-percent, mutually agreeable, creative, win-win alternative is available if we just ask and use these three questions: what is the primary issue about which we're differing, what are the goals we each seek, and what other options do we have? Ways to find common ground include finding unity amid diversity, complementing rather than opposing, agreeing on criteria for good decision-making, and sharing life-stories or faith journeys.[13]

Technological savvy is the ability to successfully navigate the world of such technologies as software, blogging, multimedia, and

---

12. For more information about these topics, see Kirkpatrick, *Communication in the Church*, 11–18.

13. For more information about these and related ways to find common ground, see Kirkpatrick, *Communication in the Church*, 72–77.

websites as tools for ministry.[14] Computers, fiber optics, and satellites create a communication superhighway. High-speed communication such as the worldwide internet, social media, and weblogs link people with information and one another. Global digital communication systems connect us to tablets, computers, and mobile devices, and our power to communicate expands through emailing, texting, browsing, webcamming, tweeting, chatting, blogging, recording, conferencing, streaming, and networking. New ethical challenges are created by global information technology, our digital cyberspace universe, and the emergence of artificial intelligence. Cyberspace ethical concerns include honesty, dehumanization, deception, privacy, social responsibility, fairness, and accessibility.[15]

Expressing appreciation is powerful. "The deepest craving of human nature is the need to be appreciated." So says philosopher and psychologist William James. It is an energy that can make our spirits soar. Appreciation is a choice we make to be thankful. It is gratitude-in-action. And it has the capacity to transform our lives by developing self-confidence, coping with change, and overcoming resentment. Appreciation motivates workers by increasing their sense of opportunity and feeling of wellbeing. Appreciation can also foster positive changes in organizations—it brings out the best in people, their organizations, and the world. Unexpressed appreciation is costly in terms of forfeiting these benefits of appreciation. Fortunately, there are skills and practices we can learn to express appreciation.[16] Encouraging effort, rewarding results, and celebrating career milestones are naturally occurring ways to express appreciation in most organizations. The way we express appreciation also matters. People respond to appreciation differently, so we need to learn their primary appreciation languages. We can

14. See the PCUSA's "Church Leadership Connection Leadership Competencies," https://www.pcusa.org/site_media/media/uploads/clc/pdfs/leadership_competencies_definitions.pdf.

15. For more information about ethics in cyberspace, see Kirkpatrick, *Communication in the Church*, 128–29.

16. See the five-step process for unleashing the power of appreciation in Kirkpatrick, *Better Ways*, 93–96.

communicate appreciation through authentic words, physical touch, quality time, acts of service, and tangible gifts.

Experiencing curiosity is apparent in the Gospel of Mark wherein Jesus often teaches by focusing on people who stay around after the crowd is gone to ask questions. He seeks people who are eager to ask questions in a safe environment, people who are lifelong learners. Our discipleship, our spiritual formation, then, is nurtured in attractive, healthy ways through cultivating curiosity. Curiosity is also a way to build relationships. Our interest in one another's interests helps us pay attention to and become acquainted with one another. Combined with humility and empathy, curiosity attracts us to each other, humility creates respect for each other, and empathy generates care for one another's wellbeing. These three practices are particularly useful when we face difficult conversations, including dealing with differences and working through disagreement and conflict with others.[17]

Character: Ways We Treat One Another

All too often, people outside the church are repelled by perceptions of judgmental and hypocritical behavior by those inside the church. This common perception is contrary to Christ's followers being welcoming, inclusive, and affirming of all people—modern day signs of Paul's teaching in Gal 3:28: "There is no longer Jew or Greek, there is no longer slave or free, there is no longer male or female; for all of you are one in Christ Jesus." Anti-racism work, partnering with Indigenous people locally and globally, and full inclusion of queer and LGBTQIA+ folks are demonstrations of this teaching, and those of us in positions of power and privilege must discover how to live into Isabel Wilkerson's charge mentioned in chapter 1: "The price of privilege is the moral duty to act when one sees another person treated unfairly. And the least that a person in the dominant caste can do is not make the pain any worse."[18]

17. For more information about these three practices, see Stewart, *Personal Communicating and Racial Equity*, 43–57.

18. Wilkerson, *Caste*, 386.

As we saw earlier, Jesus says in John 13:35, "By this everyone will know that you are my disciples, if you have love for one another." Theologically, this means that the witness to the gospel Jesus proclaimed and demonstrated is not how many souls are saved, how much prayer is practiced, or even how enthusiastic is our worship and music. No, Jesus says that it's how we treat one another in the church that draws people to our faith. *Character matters in the church!* How we live out and practice our faith is evident in Mic 6:8: "What does the Lord require of you but to do justice, and to love kindness, and to walk humbly with your God?" And in Rom 5:4–5, these poignant comments from Paul link character and hope: "Endurance produces character, and character produces hope, and hope does not disappoint us, because God's love has been poured into our hearts through the Holy Spirit that has been given to us."

Here are signs or ways we treat one another that embody healthy Christian character and behavior:

- Doing justice
- Showing kindness
- Practicing humility
- Feeling compassion
- Demonstrating love
- Promoting peace

Doing justice is centered in relationships. "Seek justice, rescue the oppressed," says Isa 1:17. Fairness in keeping obligations is central to our individual sense of justice. Social justice, on the other hand, usually refers to obligations of citizens for the common good. The goal of social justice is to create a society where no one lacks their essential needs. Doing justice, though, is more than following social norms and obligations. It is about how we treat one another. It means doing all that is necessary to create and sustain wholesome relationships with one another and to uphold everyone's dignity and rights. As Martin Luther King Jr. reminds us, "Injustice anywhere is a threat to justice everywhere." The Universal Declaration of Human Rights is the most comprehensive and global statement about our common commitment to a socially just world. It centers on providing essential needs for all people and on protecting vulnerable, marginalized, and disadvantaged groups and individuals from oppression, discrimination, and exclusion. Poverty and economic inequality undermine justice. Fortunately, great progress has been made, and we've learned how to end economic inequality and poverty. We just need to finish the journey. Achieving environmental justice, though, is proving to be elusive. Fortunately, we have strong environmental laws; unfortunately, they are all too seldom enforced. It will help to link our environmental problem-solving efforts to the fight against other social injustices such as climate change, global health, energy shortages, and women's empowerment. Fortunately, one of these other challenges, global health equity, appears achievable in our generation.[19]

Showing kindness is love in action. "Love is kind," writes Paul in 1 Cor 13:4. Loving kindly is beneficial and powerful. As Rabbi Rami Shapiro comments, "If there were a single practice capable of transforming person and planet, it would be kindness." It transforms relationships by triggering neurons in our brains that lead us to act compassionately, generously, and thoughtfully. Consequently, depression, fear, isolation, and anxiety are alleviated, resiliency from stress and fatigue increased, and positive attitudes towards us and others promoted. Prosocial behaviors are fostered while defensive and destructive behaviors are averted. Empathy is cultivated, prejudice and intolerance overcome, and listening activated. Body image is improved. Intimacy and affection are strengthened, wellbeing fostered, and longevity improved. There are many ways to show kindness, including curiosity, thoughtfulness, generosity, and pausing to guard against our hostile tendencies. Behaviors that harm relationships such as anger, defensiveness, judgment, intolerance, impatience, and threats can

---

19. For more information about doing justice, see Kirkpatrick, *Better Ways*, 103–25.

be transformed into helpful relationship behaviors such as warmth and supportiveness, openness and acceptance, patience and care. Transformative, boundless, liberating openheartedness is fostered through kindness, along with three interrelated relational qualities including compassion, joy, and equanimity.[20]

The *practice of humility* is a multifaceted positive behavior that reflects an accurate self-view, modest self-importance, and appropriate other-centeredness. "Pride makes us artificial and humility makes us real," says American Trappist monk, theologian, and social activist Thomas Merton. It finds unique expression across intellectual, political, religious, cultural, and relational contexts. Humility has a variety of benefits. It strengthens social bonds, friendships, supportiveness, mentoring, and workplace collegiality. Humble people are seen as low-maintenance, honest yet sensitive, modest, and other-oriented. Humility buffers our relationships from excessive perfectionism, competitiveness, or moralizing. It helps us cope with stress and major life transitions. It helps us more fairly evaluate information, manage conflict, and negotiate differences, and it is beneficial to societal peace such as promoting pro-environmental attitudes, decreasing bullying and aggressive behavior, and lessening delinquency and crime. Humble citizens tend to be committed to social justice, to minimize combativeness, and value diversity. We can also cultivate humility—gratitude boosts humility, as do awe-inspiring experiences through nature, beauty, or great accomplishments. Likewise, self-affirmation boosts humility by helping us cope with threatening information, accept our limitations, and diminish negative moods.

Feeling compassion is a heartfelt concern for someone's pain, unjust suffering, or unmet need. Often, though not always, our concern results in a desire to show our care in ways that help people thrive. Self-inflicted suffering and overwhelming challenges tend to lessen our motivation to show compassion. Our brains are wired to thrive on compassion—to be caring and to need caring. It helps to remember that everyone suffers, to be kind to ourselves,

---

20. For more information about showing kindness, see Kirkpatrick, *Better Ways*, 73–86.

and to practice self-compassion. Compassion is a choice we make to balance the demands compassion makes on us with the abilities and resources we need to help alleviate someone's suffering. It is also a skill to be learned, and training can cultivate our capacities for compassion. Compassion is connected to social justice by overcoming unjust suffering and promoting human flourishing individually, organizationally, and globally.

Demonstrating love is beautifully expressed in 1 Cor 13 and is summarized with these familiar words: "And now faith, hope, and love abide, these three; and the greatest of these is love" (v. 13). Not surprisingly, Paul then begins chapter 14 with these simple words: "Pursue love" (v. 1a). But what do we mean when we use the word *love*?

Rather than define *love* as a single entity, relationship scientist Ellen Berscheid suggests that we think of four kinds of love: romantic love, companionate love, compassionate love, and attachment love.[21] Romantic love is synonymous with passionate love, *eros*, and "being in love." Companionate love refers to strong liking, *philia*, or friendship love. Compassionate love is the same as *agape* and altruistic or selfless love. Finally, attachment love involves strong bonds of affection with an attachment figure. Berscheid thinks these four kinds of love differ in terms of their causes, behaviors, trajectory, and research. For example, *romantic love* arises from desirable qualities such as physical attraction, passion, or sexual desire. It expresses itself in behaviors that encourage pursuit of a sexual relationship. Its trajectory moves from uncertainty to predictability to erotic satisfaction. A great deal of research on close relationships focuses on romantic love in comparison to the other three kinds of love.

Companionate love is caused by similarity, proximity, and familiarity with others. It includes enjoyable interactions, spending time together, sharing similar interests, and expressing liking. While it may take time to develop and be long-lasting, it may also

---

21. See Fehr, "Social Psychology of Love," 202–3. For more information on Berscheid's conception of love, see her articles "Love in the Fourth Dimension" and "Searching for the Meaning of 'Love.'"

become important quickly and change when partners and circumstances change. While friendship-based love is a long-recognized concept, little empirical research exists to date. Friendship-based love is related to *agape* love as expressed in 1 Cor 13.

Compassionate love, though, is most closely associated with Paul's use of *agape* love in 1 Cor 13. It is triggered by someone in need or distress, and behaviors vary depending on the nature of the stress detected. It may develop early in a relationship although it endures when tested or even when sacrifices are necessary over an extended period of time. While the subject of recent empirical studies, most research work focuses on non-intimate relationships such as strangers and doctor-patient contexts.

Attachment love is occasioned by a threatening situation and acts that promote proximity. Whereas a great deal is known about attachment theory, styles, and orientations, it has only recently been studied as a kind of love.

Promoting peace is what Jesus is getting at in his Beatitudes in the Sermon on the Mount when he teaches: "Blessed are the peacemakers, for they will be called children of God" (Matt 5:9). Peacemaking is really an alternative way of relating to one another to avoidance or passivity, on the one hand, and aggression or violence, on the other hand. Earlier we learned that forgiveness joins truth and justice to produce peace. We see these dynamics at work in the way Jesus handles the rift between an adulterous woman and her unscrupulous accusers who think she should be stoned to death in John 7:53—8:11. Jesus promotes peace by transforming the situation when he raises the issue about who is without sin. He says to let the person without sin cast the first stone. He slows down the whole situation and buys time to discover a fresh, imaginative, peaceful option. He offers the crowd a life-saving alternative to repent of their actions—they may turn around and walk away. He then restores the woman's dignity by asking her where her accusers are. Seeing none, Jesus sets her free from condemnation to turn around and start a new life. Truth is served—her sin, as well as those of her accusers, are exposed. Justice is served—all face the consequences of their sin. All are invited to follow the right path: to go and sin no more. Consequently, Jesus's forgiving spirit and actions promote peace in this situation by wedding truth and justice.

Both avoidance and violence are also often a result of mistrust and communication breakdowns. Dialogue builds relationships, creates trust, overcomes fears, and bridges walls that divide us. It promotes peaceful and just relationships between people and nations. Moreover, biblical scholar, theologian, and activist Walter Wink suggests that Jesus introduces what he calls a "third way" to promote peace as an alternative to the ways of passivity and violence, of avoidance and aggression. This third way, *assertive nonviolence*, promotes peace wherein "going the second mile" exposes oppression, "turning the other cheek" is an act of defiance, and impoverished debtors use the system against itself.[22]

Collaboration: Ways We Work with One Another

Collaboration has to do with ways we partner with one another—ways we work together. Elsewhere, I've commented: "In our postmodern, post-Christian, post-denominational era, people are often more receptive to and interested in practicing collaborative leadership than people in previous generations. For congregations in the Reformed tradition that value 'the priesthood of all believers,' collaborative partnering between clergy and laity is a long-valued best practice. Nonetheless, the top-down, corporate model of directive leadership is common in many quarters. While some people may resist the movement from top-down to collaborative leadership, this shift will be particularly beneficial for decision-making and leading meetings in congregations."[23]

Leadership competencies are particularly important to congregations when they are seeking a new pastor. In the Presbyterian Church (USA), for example, pastor-nominating committees searching for a new pastor identify leadership competencies they

---

22. For further explanation of Jesus's third way and identification of modern-day followers, see Wink, *Powers That Be*, 111.
23. Kirkpatrick, *Communication in the Church*, 49–50.

hope to find matched in pastoral candidates they'll be considering. They select ten of the thirty-three competencies listed in chapter 2 from among these four categories: six theological/spiritual interpreter competencies, five communication competencies, fifteen organizational leadership competencies, and seven interpersonal engagement competencies. A church pastor nominating committee for whom I was a denominational liaison selected the following ten competencies they hoped to find in a pastor:

- Compassionate
- Preaching and Worship Leadership
- Spiritual Maturity
- Public Communicator
- Technologically Savvy
- Willingness to Engage Conflict
- Organizational Agility
- Strategy and Vision
- Collaboration
- Interpersonal Engagement

Rarely do the ten competencies a candidate selects match all ten competencies a congregation selects. Rather, pastor nominating committees hope to find at least five, if not six or more matching competencies in candidates they'll be considering. Fortunately, there are other factors to consider such as a candidate's experience, successes, the type of call they're seeking, areas of growth, and ability to lead change. Statements of faith, references, salary expectations, and sermon links are also essential.

For our purposes, signs of healthy collaboration in the church are evident in such ways we work together as the following:

- Strategizing and visioning
- Discerning and decision-making
- Openness to change

- Organizational agility
- Engagement of spiritual gifts
- Partnering

Strategizing and visioning is future-oriented. It looks ahead clearly; focuses on big-picture challenges and emerging opportunities; helps anticipate future consequences and trends accurately; and it creates a compelling and inspired vision for its preferred future. It sees possibilities and generates strategies to accomplish the mission and goals that are established. Emotions and thoughts provide complementary functions in how we process information. Comments pastor, therapist, educator, and leadership consultant Peter Steinke, "Emotional forces work best in emergencies, and thought serves best when understanding and planning are needed."[24] For example, emotional reactions are prominent when we are in survival mode, while rationally driven reactions move us along to a thriving orientation. He also suggests that positive outcomes emerge when leadership is "centered in principle, based on self-regulation, and anchored by thoughtful positions. Principle provides clarity, self-regulation helps to avoid extremes, and thoughtful positions lead to necessary action."[25]

Discerning and decision-making require wisdom and contextualization to enable congregations to gain clear direction and to thrive. Spiritual and theological depth, biblical grounding, and prayerful engagement of the Holy Spirit's guidance are prominent. It requires the ability to access accurately the congregation's mission opportunities, to draw wisdom from its history, and to determine its uniqueness as a congregation. It is aware of the long-term implications of choices made, generates solutions, and makes midterm corrections. Discernment and decision-making balance analysis, spirituality, wisdom, experience, and judgment. A major gift from Ignatian spirituality is its wisdom about discernment. From this tradition, "discernment enables us to assess situations, pay attention to various clues, approach our decision making

24. Steinke, *Uproar*, 142.
25. Steinke, *Uproar*, 59.

prayerfully, and ultimately choose well according to our faith and our life situation."[26]

As we'll discover in the recurring themes and conclusions from our research project, *openness to change* is a highly rated sign of both congregational hope and health. Congregations need receptivity to change to adapt to a world in flux, to discern new and emerging forms of ministry, and to discover hopeful and healthy ways to accomplish their goals and live into their vision and mission. It also helps attract and assimilate new members into our congregation's life and ministry. Change agents, both lay and clergy, are needed to help congregations discern a compelling vision and decide which mission strategies to adopt and implement. Persons with the courage to comfortably handle the risks and uncertainties necessary to accomplish goals are needed—people who can think creatively and are not afraid to challenge the status quo. Resilience that learns from failure and adversity is required, as is noticing needed changes to personal, interpersonal, organizational, and leadership behaviors. Dealing well with ambiguity is necessary to cope effectively with change, as are appropriate feedback, regret, and midcourse corrections. Consultant, coach, and spiritual director Susan Beaumont offers hope for our in-between times in her book *How to Lead When You Don't Know Where You're Going: Leading in a Liminal Season*. She offers practical wisdom about leading with presence, tending the soul of the institution, deepening group discernment, shaping institutional memory, clarifying purpose, and engaging emergence.[27]

Organizational agility refers to knowing how organizations work and how to get things done through formal and informal channels. It embraces nimble and innovative ways of working together. It requires understanding the importance of crafting and following good organizational and personnel policies, practices,

---

26. See Wright, "Discernment at Different Stages of Life," https://www.ignatianspirituality.com/discernment-different-stages-life.

27. See Beaumont, *How to Lead*, v. See also Rendle, *Leading Change in the Congregation*. Related sources on managing transitions include Mann, *The In-Between Church*, and Bridges, *Managing Transitions*.

and procedures. It also acknowledges the importance of using power appropriately, of keeping appropriate boundaries, of bridging cultures, and of political savvy. It keeps us informed about proper church governance and maintains current laws, regulations, trends, and developments both internally and externally. It fosters healthy relationships required to ensure the integrity of the organization. Finally, it holds leaders and members accountable to accomplish their responsibilities in a timely manner, within budget, and with appropriate measurable outcomes.

Engagement of spiritual gifts is informed by this teaching of Paul in 1 Cor 12:4–7: "Now there are varieties of gifts, but the same Spirit; and there are varieties of services, but the same Lord; and there are varieties of activities, but it is the same God who activates all of them in everyone. To each is given the manifestation of the Spirit for the common good." He goes on to name such gifts as those of apostleship, prophecy, teaching, deeds of power, gifts of healing, forms of assistance, and forms of leadership. As we've noted earlier, a helpful way of looking at spiritual gifts is in terms of big-picture leadership competencies in congregations, including gifts of theological and spiritual interpretation, communication, organizational leadership, and interpersonal engagement.

The practice of *partnering*, in contrast to that of directing, is evident in 1 Pet 5:1–4 where Peter describes a servant-leadership model: "Now as an elder myself and a witness of the sufferings of Christ, as well as one who shares in the glory to be revealed, I exhort the elders among you to tend the flock of God that is in your charge, exercising the oversight, not under compulsion but willingly, as God would have you do it—not for sordid gain but eagerly. Do not lord it over those in your charge, but be examples to the flock. And when the chief shepherd appears, you will win the crown of glory that never fades." Indeed, leaders have significant impact on how other members of an organization face and manage challenges. Why, though, must effective leadership flow through the person at the top? Why, for example, depend on their calm presence and courageous behavior to trickle down? Why not view leadership as a collaborative effort or partnership among all team members?[28] For congregations whose theological convictions affirm "the priesthood of all believers," collaborative partnering between laity and clergy is a long-valued best practice. In this view of leadership, for example, leaders work not only on staying calm and having courage themselves, but also work to facilitate calm and courage among all members of their organization. In other words, everyone is invited to join in creating healthy, flourishing relationships and maturely functioning, transformative organizations.

SUMMARY

Chapter 2 presented a wide array of ways healthy congregations have been conceived, categorized and created over the years. Now, in chapter 3, we have introduced a new and fully developed relational perspective based on the 4 C's framework as signs of healthy congregations. An important question remains: how are our congregations doing in each of these areas? We can now test the validity of these signs of healthy congregations as measures of congregational health. In the next chapter, chapter 4, you'll find the design of an empirical research project to test the validity and usefulness of our new 4 C's relational perspective, including the twenty-four signs of congregational health. Results of this empirical research are presented, including observations, discussion, and conclusions. Also, guidelines to create hope-filled and healthy futures for mainline churches are found in chapter 5.

28. In *Communication in the Church*, 35–36, I point out that most congregations designate someone to help a group work as a team to accomplish its task. I define a leader as a member of the group designated to help the group go where it wants to go to the extent that such help is needed. Viewed this way, leadership is a function to perform rather than a person at the top. Most congregational leaders have little authority to "call the shots." Group members want a say in what the group does and how they participate. They think of the group as "theirs" rather than the leader's, and they expect leaders to be a partner, not a person in charge. I also see leadership functioning on a sliding scale, depending on the extent to which a group needs direction and facilitation. One person, the designated leader, may provide this leadership, or several members may share it. Ideally, everyone shares in helping the group work as a team and accomplish its task.

SIGNS OF HEALTHY CONGREGATIONS
PRACTICAL APPLICATIONS

1. From "not well" to "very well," assess how your congregation creates Christian community. How about in the following ways: build relationships, affirm and support one another, trust one another, show empathy, practice forgiveness, and bridge cultures? What insights about creating community in your congregation can you take away from these assessments?

2. From "not well" to "very well," assess how people in your congregation communicate with one another. How about in the following ways: engage conflict, listen to one another, find common ground, use technology, express appreciation, and exercise curiosity? What insights about how people communicate with one another in your congregation can you take away from these assessments?

3. From "not well" to "very well," assess how people in your congregation treat one another. How about in the following ways: do justice, show kindness, practice humility, feel compassion, demonstrate love, and promote peace? What insights about how people treat one another in your congregation can you take away from these assessments?

4. From "not well" to "very well," assess how people in your congregation work together. How about in the following ways: strategize and vision, discern and make decisions, be open to change, be agile organizationally, engage members' spiritual gifts, and partner and work collaboratively? What insights about how people work together in your congregation can you take away from these assessments?

Note: These four questions are included in the empirical research project described in chapter 4 to test the validity and usefulness of signs of healthy congregations presented in this chapter.

FOR FURTHER STUDY

Beaumont, Susan. *How to Lead When You Don't Know Where You're Going: Leading in a Liminal Season.* Lanham, MD: Roman & Littlefield, 2019.

Kirkpatrick, Thomas G. *Better Ways to Better Relationships in the Church: Guidelines for Practicing Humility, Experiencing Empathy, Feeling Compassion, Showing Kindness, Expressing Appreciation, and Doing Justice.* Eugene, OR: Wipf & Stock, 2021.

———. *Communication in the Church: A Handbook for Healthier Relationships.* Lanham, MD: Rowman & Littlefield, 2016.

Steinke, Peter L. *Uproar: Calm Leadership in Anxious Times.* Lanham, MD: Rowman & Littlefield, 2019.

Wink, Walter. *The Powers That Be: Theology for a New Millennium.* Minneapolis: Augsburg, 1998.

4

Research Project

IN CHAPTER 1, WE learned that hope is goal-directed and requires willpower and waypower. Then chapter 2 presents eighteen ways researchers and practitioners understand what makes congregations alive, vital, thriving, healthy, and flourishing. And in chapter 3, we learned about a new way to understand healthy congregations: a 4 C's relational perspective. This 4 C's approach identifies signs of healthy congregations in terms of community, communication, character, and collaboration.

To test hypotheses about signs of hope and health in mainline churches, including our new 4 C's relational approach to congregational health, a research project was designed and completed.

See appendix 1 for the research design, including seven hypotheses, research questions, and signs of hope and health questionnaires for denominational leaders and pastors created to test the hypotheses and answer research questions.

In this chapter, you'll find questionnaire results for denominational leaders and for pastors, observations and discussion, and conclusions.

QUESTIONNAIRE RESULTS FOR DENOMINATIONAL LEADERS

Fifty-seven of five hundred denominational leaders submitted responses to the Signs of Hope and Health Questionnaire. Returns include 21 of 134 Presbyterian executive presbyters, 15 of 144 United Methodist district superintendents, 7 of 90 Episcopal bishops, 5 of 65 Lutheran bishops, 5 of 34 United Church of Christ conference ministers, and 4 of 33 American Baptist executive ministers. These responses represent slightly more than an 11 percent overall return rate, a fairly typical questionnaire response rate. While I did refer these leaders to my website for further information about my background and publications, I am an unknown researcher and writer to most of these leaders and not associated with a research institution. Nonetheless, clear themes and striking and notable responses emerged.

Responses to the four open-ended questions created to test hypothesis 2 do indeed provide fresh signs of hope and health from our denominational leaders. Appendix 3 reports recurring themes with several striking and notable responses,[1] as well as some borderline responses. Striking responses include "spiritual life" as a healthy sign and "unwillingness to change" and "me-focused" as least hopeful signs. "Working together" and "mission-focused" as hopeful signs and "strong leadership" as a condition in which hope thrives are notable responses. And borderline responses include "outreach" and "willingness to change" as hopeful signs, "mission-focused" and "strong leadership" as healthy signs, and "spiritual life" and "mission-focused" conditions in which hope thrives.

Responses to the three questions about hope (see hypothesis 1), the eight questions about healthy congregations (see hypothesis 3), and the 4 C's questions (see hypothesis 4) confirm that hopeful and healthy congregations do "well" or "fairly well" on all these

---

1. Striking responses are those cited by 60 percent or more respondents, notable responses by 40 percent to 50 percent, and borderline responses by 35 percent to 40 percent.

measures.[2] And as for the two optional questions rating congregational hope and health (see hypothesis 5), results were considerably higher than expected for health (70 percent "healthy" or "very healthy" rather than 33 percent). While not predicted, results were rated even higher for hope (80 percent "hopeful" or "very hopeful"). Appendix 5 reports these results.

QUESTIONNAIRE RESULTS FOR PASTORS

Twenty-two of 108 pastors submitted responses to the Signs of Hope and Health Questionnaires, slightly more than a 20 percent return rate. Returns include 9 of 44 pastors of healthy congregations, 4 of 39 pastors of hopeful congregations, 6 of 24 pastors of both hopeful and healthy congregations, and 3 of 4 pastors in the pretest. While this is nearly double the return rate for denominational leaders, the sample size is relatively small. Nonetheless, as with denominational leaders, clear themes and striking and notable responses emerged.

As with denominational leaders, pastors provide fresh signs of hope and health. Appendix 4 reports striking, notable, and borderline responses to our four open-ended questions about hope and health to test hypothesis 2. Spiritual life is especially striking as a sign of health. Also striking responses for pastors are mission-focused and outreach as hopeful signs and spiritual life as a condition in which hope thrives. Notable responses include working together as a hopeful sign; unwillingness to change and me-focused as least hopeful signs; mission-focused as a condition in which hope thrives; and mission-focused as a healthy sign. Working together as a healthy sign is a borderline response for pastors.

Appendix 6 presents questionnaire results for pastors on the questions about hope, health, and the 4 C's. Responses from pastors of hopeful, healthy, and both hopeful and healthy congregations all

---

2. These responses use a standard of 5.5 to 6.0 on a scale of 1 to 6 to mean "excellent or very well," 4.5 to 5.4 to mean "well," 3.5 to 4.4 to mean "fairly well," 2.5 to 3.4 to mean "average or neither well nor poor," and 1 to 2.4 to mean "very poor or not well."

confirm that hopeful and healthy congregations do "well" or "fairly well" on overall health along with the other fourteen measures.

Finally, appendix 7 reveals confirmation of our expectations in hypothesis 6 that people in hopeful, healthy, and both hopeful and healthy congregations do "well" or "fairly well" on all twenty-four measures of how they create Christian community, communicate with one another, treat one another, and work with one another.

OBSERVATIONS AND DISCUSSION

Hypothesis 1: Hopeful congregations will do well in finding ways to set and meet their goals, energetically pursue their goals, and solve problems even when people get discouraged.

Denominational leaders affirm that hopeful churches in their regions are doing "well" (ranging from 4.7 to 4.9) in each of the three measures of hope. The same is true for pastors of hopeful and healthy congregations (with responses totals ranging from 4.6 to 5.0). Also, it is worth noting that while these congregations do these activities well, they do none either poorly or exceptionally well. See Appendices 5 and 6 for these results.

Pastors of congregations that are both hopeful and healthy report considerably higher ratings on these three activities (5.2 to 5.5) than pastors of either hopeful (4.5 to 4.8) or healthy (4.3 to 4.9) congregations. Perhaps being both hopeful and healthy creates a synergy that elevates their hopeful activity ratings. Bolstering this possible phenomenon is the counter-intuitive observation that healthy congregations have a lower overall health rating (4.5) then their overall hope rating (4.9). Finally, it is intriguing that congregations that are both hopeful and healthy do well on overall hope (4.7) but have considerably higher overall health ratings (5.3). We will also explore these results in hypothesis 7.

RESEARCH PROJECT

Hypothesis 2: Both denominational leaders and pastors will provide fresh signs of hope and signs of health in mainline churches.

Many signs of hope and health occurred multiple times. These similar responses were grouped or categorized, and then each group was named or identified by theme. The percentage of times a particular theme was cited by the number of respondents was then calculated. These percentages are reported for fifty-seven denominational leaders and for twenty-two pastors in Appendices 3 and 4.

Fresh signs of hope and health appear as very striking, notable, or borderline responses from the recurring themes derived from questionnaire responses by denominational leaders (see appendix 3) and pastors (see appendix 4). Using a standard of 60 percent and higher for a striking response, 40 percent to 59 percent a notable response, and 35 percent to 39 percent borderline responses, there are three striking responses, three notable responses, and six borderline responses for denominational leaders. For pastors, four responses are striking, five are notable, and one borderline.

To summarize our findings for denominational leaders, then, two of the three striking responses are least hopeful signs (unwillingness to change and me-focused) and the third is a healthy sign (spiritual life). Two notable responses are most hopeful signs (working together and mission-focused) and the third is a hopeful sign of thriving (strong leadership). Finally, borderline responses include two healthy signs (mission-focused and strong leadership), two most hopeful signs (outreach and willingness to change), and two hopeful signs of thriving (spiritual life and mission-focused).

For pastors, the four striking responses include mission-focused and outreach as most hopeful signs, spiritual life as a condition in which hope thrives, and spiritual life as a sign of health. The five notable responses are working together as most hopeful, unwilling to change and me-focused as least hopeful, mission-focused as hope thrives, and mission-focused as a healthy sign. Working together as a healthy sign is the borderline response.

Let's look a little more closely at these twelve responses as fresh signs of hope and health for denominational leaders. *Change* is prominent with willingness to change a healthy sign and unwillingness to change a least hopeful sign. *Focus* matters mightily with me-focused a least hopeful sign and mission-focused a three-peat: a healthy sign, hopeful sign, and hopeful sign of thriving. *Leadership* is key as a hopeful sign of thriving and a healthy sign. Finally, *spiritual life* is featured as a healthy sign and hopeful sign of thriving.

As signs of hope, then, *change, focus, leadership,* and *spiritual life* are all prominent features. And as signs of health, *change, focus, leadership,* and *spiritual life* are likewise all central features. In summary, spiritual life and mission-focused are the most prominent themes, with willingness to change and leadership notable. These four themes are fresh signs of both hope and health in mainline churches according to the denominational leader respondents who participated in this research project.

Here's a cross-section sampling of denominational leader responses that led to the identification of our four themes (denominational leader's denomination in parenthesis):

Change

> "A willingness to try something new, even if it fails; a spirit of openness and inclusivity." (UCC)

> "An unwillingness to try or go outside comfort zones, yet still expect things to change regardless. An unhealthy or unrealistic dependency on others to solve problems for them." (Episcopal)

> "People with imagination that think out of the box." (PCUSA)

> "No desire to try anything risky. Desire to go back to the way things were in the 'glory' days rather than face the issues at hand boldly." (ABC)

"Congregations that are open and welcoming, open and welcoming to diversity of ideas and opinions, and believe that God is working through them to make a difference in the world and are doing it." (UM)

Focus

"Addressing what breaks God's heart in their communities." (PCUSA)

"Some faith communities have a local food ministry program that may be the only type of church some folks experience. Others are leading racial justice and healing efforts in their community along with cross-cultural ministry collaborations." (Episcopal)

"Many congregations are engaging in community service and caring ministries to foster children and foster parents, food-based ministries like food banks or free meals, new mother and baby ministries, and community cleanup projects." (ABC)

"Partnerships with local schools, community organizations, and other churches to serve their neighborhoods, such as food, clothing, and housing." (PCUSA)

Leadership

"A leader who remains resilient and hopeful in the midst of challenges. Healthy communication in the congregation." (ELCA)

"Determination to accept the challenges of the world around us and leadership that can focus on how to meet those challenges." (PCUSA)

"Passionate pastors who encourage the passions and gifts of laity. Openness to new ways of being in ministry." (UM)

"Church members have a voice and share leadership in open, inclusive, and enthusiastic ways." (PCUSA)

Spiritual Life

"A core of spiritual individuals whose spirituality is nourished by the congregation." (Episcopal)

"Creating a new worship experience specifically oriented toward individuals who feel excluded or rejected by traditional church experiences." (PCUSA)

"Are engaging with the community to address racial justice, homelessness, housing, and environmental issues. These churches have taken their discipleship into their communities testifying about their faith in Jesus by being witnesses of Jesus's teachings." (UM)

"Love and compassion ripple through their relationships and they are open to change. They trust that God is 'doing a new thing' to which they are called to participate. They know when to grieve and lament and they know when to celebrate and rejoice." (PCUSA)

For the ten responses as fresh signs of hope and health for pastors, *focus* appears highly on all four lists: as a striking hopeful sign, as notable healthy and hope thrives signs, and as a notable me-focused least hopeful sign. *Spiritual life* ranks highest on both the health and hope thrives lists. *Working together* makes all four lists with one notable hopeful and a borderline healthy sign. *Change* appears on the three hope lists, although it is less prominent with only unwilling to change a notable least hopeful sign.

For pastors, then, recurring themes center on *focus, spiritual life, working together,* and *change*. Spiritual life, mission-focused, and outreach are prominent themes, working together notable, and willingness to change a notable but less prominent theme. These features are like those we observed for denominational leaders, although for pastors, outreach joins mission-focused, and working together replaces the theme of leadership for denominational leaders. In sum, spiritual life and focus on mission and outreach are most prominent themes, with working together and willingness to change notable. These four themes are fresh signs of both hope and health according to our pastor participants.

Here's a cross-section sampling of pastor responses that led to the identification of our four themes (pastor's denomination in parenthesis):

Change

> "The congregation and its leaders are very creative and willing to take risks." (PCUSA)

> "Congregations that have decided to insulate themselves from the community in which they are situated. They are unwilling to change so that those in the community would feel welcomed and at home in the church." (Episcopal)

Focus

> "When we are serving the larger community outside the walls of our church. When our music programs connect people to one another and the divine and attract people outside our church membership." (PCUSA)

> "A church that is focused outward on the community and is welcoming to newcomers and helps them get connected." (Episcopal)

> "The congregation is active and engaged and they participate in the life of the larger community." (Episcopal)

Working Together

"A desire to work together on tasks." (UM)

"A staff that gets along with a great deal of teamwork, and leaders who are evenhanded and open minded." (UM)

"Leaders strive to increase transparency of decision making and build trust among members." (UM)

Spiritual Life

"Spirit-filled worship that changes things up every now and then. The familiar order and liturgy undergird the flow of worship still and make room for the Spirit to flow in testimonies and opportunities to share stories and prayer requests." (PCUSA)

"Living out our faith in caring for others and good stewardship of our resources are spiritual practices that lead to life-long discipleship." (PCUSA)

For a case study featuring ways these recurring themes are evident in a hopeful and healthy small-sized congregation, see appendix 8.

Finally, here's how the pastor of a hopeful and healthy mid-sized congregation illustrates ways they create hope and health in each of our four recurring themes:

"Focus on mission and outreach and working together are probably the greatest sources of hope in our congregation. By serving our community, we find that the community members are transformed, but also that we are transformed in the process by the hope of making a difference in the world. We come together to serve, and a sense of unity and fellowship is nurtured despite whatever else may be going on in the world, in our nation, and even in our community. We can overcome differences by uniting around service and mission. Every summer, we pack sack lunches every Sunday after worship for four weeks. We call this 'Open Table.' This ensures that students who receive free and reduced lunches during the school year can still get food during the summer. This has been a very effective ministry at uniting our congregation and sparking hope among our members, knowing that we are working together to feed hungry children. Even though members of my church may disagree about the politics of welfare, we can all agree that children shouldn't go hungry over the summer, so we bond over making peanut butter and jelly sandwiches knowing that those will feed kids who need it."

Hypothesis 3: People in healthy congregations do well in their leadership, biblical and theological anchoring, Christian formation, worship, mission and outreach, welcome, and finances.

With responses from denominational leaders ranging between 4.5 to 5.2 (see appendix 5) on these baseline activities of healthy churches, these results reveal that healthy congregations do, in fact, do well on all seven of these activities. It is also worth noting that none of these activities are rated either poorly or exceptionally well. Healthy congregations, then, do well overall in these bedrock areas of their life and ministry, as predicted. Responses from pastors are nearly identical, ranging from 4.5 to 5.3 (see appendix 6). Congregations that are both hopeful and healthy do considerably better overall (5.3) than hopeful (4.5) and healthy (4.3) congregations. It is worth noting that mission and outreach in these congregations received the only perfect mark (6.0) among all questionnaire responses. In fact, it was half a point higher than any other activity.

For an example of responses to the Signs of Hope and Health Questionnaire from the pastor of a midsized hopeful and healthy congregation in assessing how well people in his congregation do in these seven activities, see the case study in appendix 9.

Here's how the pastor of this congregation illustrates how some of these areas are creating health in the congregation:

"Financial stability allows the church to focus on ministry and mission. When we balanced our budget, the next year our leadership council was able to think creatively and generously about where we could invest our available resources instead of just making sure we were paying our bills. Welcoming new people has also created health in our congregation. We have added 150 members in the last 7 years. Those new members bring new ideas, energy, and vitality to our church family. The act of welcoming these new members provides an opportunity for our current members to practice a ministry of hospitality, which also contributes to the health of the church. Our old members visit our new members and bring them flowers after they join the church, which not only lets them get to know the new members, but also builds up the church. The old members get to be reminded about what they love about the church as they share with the new members in these interactions."

Hypothesis 4: People in hopeful and healthy congregations do well in creating a sense of community, in communicating with one another, in the way they treat one another, and in working with one another.

In the test of our 4 C's relational perspective about healthy congregations presented in chapter 3, results are promising. As appendix 5 reveals, for denominational leaders, people in healthy congregations do well in character (how they treat one another, 4.9), community (creating Christian community, 4.9), collaboration (working with one another, 4.5), and fairly well in communication (communicating with one another, 4.3). Note that these congregations do better in character and community than in collaboration and communication.

As evident in appendix 6, for pastors, all congregations do well on all four measures, ranging from 4.5 to 5.2, although they do better in character (5.2) and collaboration (5.2) than in community (4.8) and much better than in communication (4.5). For an example of responses to the Signs of Hope and Health

Questionnaire from the pastor of a midsized hopeful and healthy congregation in assessing how well people in his congregation do on these four measures, see the case study in appendix 9.

Here is how the pastor of this congregation illustrates ways it creates community:

> "Creating Christian community focused on building God's kingdom is the heartbeat of our church. We do that well through both fellowship events and through opportunities for our church to serve together, side by side. We have started new fellowship events in the last few years like a night at the local summer league semi-pro baseball team. We meet ahead of time in a park near the field and share a meal and then go to the game together. It's a chance to interact in a less formal environment than the church that builds up community. We also held a 'food truck roundup' event in our parking lot that brought out church members and community members. We had three food trucks park and set up picnic tables, yard games, and music. The informal chance to break bread and share some fun together brought us closer together as a Christian community, while also expanding our reach to the larger community and inviting them to join us."

This congregation also realized it needs to improve its communication with the larger community. Like many congregations, they often use language that is understood by insiders but is foreign to outsiders. So, when they are trying to communicate with the larger community, they make sure they are using language that is understandable. For example, when they buy ads in the paper to invite the community to church events, they are careful about what words they are using so that they are both understandable and welcoming. Inviting the community to a "Lenten" concert is confusing, so they just call it a "Winter" concert.

We will be examining twenty-four specific ways these 4 C's are evident as measures of relational health in questionnaires to pastors of congregations identified as healthy, hopeful, and both hopeful and healthy in hypothesis 6.

Hypothesis 5: Denominational leaders will report that around one-third of congregations in their region are healthy.

Results indicate that denominational leaders are much more optimistic about the healthiness of their congregations than expected. In fact, as evident in appendix 5, they rate half their congregations as healthy, about 20 percent as very healthy, and only about 20 percent as not very healthy. In other words, far more of their congregations are perceived as healthy or very healthy (around 70 percent) than not very healthy (20 percent). They also believe their congregations are doing fairly well in overall health (3.5).

Likewise, denominational leaders are very optimistic about how hopeful they are about their congregations. They are hopeful for about 60 percent of their congregations and very hopeful for about 20 percent. This 80 percent hopeful rating contrasts sharply with only about 15 percent perceived as not very hopeful.

Overall health and hope measures for pastors reveal that all their congregations are doing well (4.8 for hope and 4.7 for health), as evident in appendix 6, although congregations both hopeful and healthy have a considerably higher health rating (5.3).

These unexpectedly high healthiness ratings are among the most eye-catching of this research project's findings. Impressive as well are the even higher overall hopefulness marks, and the finding that congregations that are both hopeful and healthy have considerably higher healthiness ratings than those for hopeful and for healthy congregations is especially noteworthy. Apparently, being both hopeful and healthy matters!

Hypothesis 6: People in healthy congregations do well in experiencing sets of six ways they create Christian community, communicate with one another, treat one another, and work with one another.

To gain more in-depth information about our 4 C's than denominational leaders can provide, pastors of congregations identified by denominational leaders as most hopeful and most healthy were asked how well people in their congregations do in twenty-four specific ways they create community, communicate, treat one another, and work together (six specific ways for each of our 4 C's).

As evident in appendix 7, all twenty-four practical ways to exemplify the 4 C's are done well or fairly well for all congregations, averaging 4.9 combined for the six measures of character and 4.7 for the eighteen measures of collaboration, community, and communication. For collaboration, partnering (5.1) and discerning and decision-making (5.0) are rated highest, and organizational agility (4.4) and strategizing and visioning (4.3) lowest. Showing kindness (5.3), demonstrating love (5.2), and feeling compassion (5.1) are highest and doing justice (4.3) lowest as measures of character. Showing empathy (5.4) and building relationships (5.0) show up highest for community and bridging cultures (4.1) lowest. Finally, finding common ground (5.1) and expressing appreciation (5.0) appear at the top and engaging conflict (4.0) at the bottom for communication.

Overall, then, nine of these combined measures are rated 5.0 or above, three for character and two each for collaboration, community, and communication. With ratings from 5.0 to 5.4, none of these combined high-ranking measures stand out—all are in the same range. However, seven measures are rated "very well" (5.5 to 5.8) for congregations that are both hopeful and health: showing kindness, 5.8; partnering, finding common ground, and showing empathy, all 5.7; and discerning and decision-making, demonstrating love, and building relationships, all 5.5. At the other end of the spectrum and rated well below all other combined measures of relational health are engaging in conflict, 4.0; bridging cultures, 4.1; doing justice, 4.3; strategizing and visioning, 4.3; organizational agility, 4.4; and practicing forgiveness, 4.4.

In view of the value of being both hopeful and healthy just noted above, these seven measures should not surprise us. In fact, they pinpoint particular ways these congregations are particularly healthy: in community through building relationships and showing empathy; in communication through finding common ground; in character through showing kindness and demonstrating love;

and in collaboration through discussion and decision-making and partnering. Should hopeful congregations and healthy congregations wish to strengthen their overall relational health, they might consider these seven particular ways as starting points.

Further, congregations that would like to become more relationally healthy might assess and work on how they engage conflict, bridge cultures, do justice, strategize and vision, be agile organizationally, and practice forgiveness.

For example, one 100-member congregation became more intentional about bridging cultures in its community by broadening its mission statement ("Serving Christ by building an inclusive community that helps one another understand, experience, and reflect God's love") and now expresses it this way: "We are an all-inclusive church, offering a safe, peaceful, and welcoming environment to all who seek solace, comfort, and fellowship within the body of Christ. We specifically welcome those from LGBTQ+ communities, and from all nationalities, religions, and ethnicities. As our building is a safe space, we strictly disallow all forms of discriminatory speech or action within it." This statement is posted on the church's entryway doors and on the front of its worship bulletins.

Another congregation experienced an especially painful interpersonal conflict among several leaders and decided to change the way it engages conflict. This 250-member congregation is no different than most congregations in facing conflict from time to time. This time, though, was different. What began as a huge breakdown in communication sparked a conflict that really needed to be addressed in person instead of in emails flying back and forth. A ministry team leader felt bullied by an email from several council members into using ministry team funds inappropriately. The email contained inflammatory and below-the-belt comments that were never owned and did not land well with the team leader. Rather than getting together to work out their differences, the team leader filed a formal complaint and demanded an apology. When an apology was eventually forthcoming, the team leader felt it was insincere and inadequate. Things spiraled out of control and over time blew up into a major, damaging, and hurtful encounter, eventually resulting in all three parties leaving the church. This traumatic, unfortunate conflict episode led the council to take a hard look at how the congregation engages in conflict. So, it invited a conflict management consultant to conduct two workshop sessions, the first with an overview of healthy conflict engagement guidelines and the second with opportunity to practice effective listening and conflict management skills. The sessions were well attended by thirty-five to forty people with various leadership roles in the congregation. A lasting impact from the workshops is a commitment to address differences openly, directly, and constructively and to use newly acquired communication tools to prevent the root of conflict from simmering in the background.

For an example of responses to the Signs of Hope and Health Questionnaire from the pastor of a midsized hopeful and healthy congregation in assessing how well people in his congregation do on these twenty-four measures of community, communication, character, and collaboration, see the case study in appendix 9.

Hypothesis 7: Hopeful congregations also tend to be healthy congregations and vice versa.

As appendix 6 confirms, hopeful, healthy, and both hopeful and healthy congregations all indeed do well in both their overall hope and overall health ratings. Hopeful congregations have a slightly higher overall hope rating (4.5) than their overall health rating (4.3). However, in our observations and discussion of hypothesis 1, we noted the counterintuitive phenomenon that healthy congregations have a lower overall health rating (4.5) than their overall hope rating (4.9). We also noted the phenomenon that congregations that are both hopeful and healthy do well on their overall hope rating (4.7) but considerably higher on overall health (5.3).

As predicted, then, hopeful congregations do well in both hope and health. Perhaps it is not surprising that they are slightly more hopeful than healthy. While we've confirmed that congregations identified as both hopeful and healthy are indeed both hopeful and healthy, it is intriguing that they are considerably more healthy than hopeful. More research to better understand this phenomenon is warranted. Perplexing, though, is our observation that healthy congregations, while both healthy and hopeful, are more hopeful than healthy. Again, more research is necessary to determine if this is an anomalous finding or if other dynamics are a work.

CONCLUSIONS

1. Hopeful and healthy congregations make hope happen by setting and meeting goals, energetically pursuing goals, and solving problems even when people get discouraged. Congregations that are both hopeful and healthy are better at these three hopeful activities than either hopeful or healthy congregations.

2. For denominational leaders, signs of hope and health center on willingness to change, mission-focus, spiritual life, and leadership. For pastors, signs of hope and health center on willingness to change, mission-focus and outreach, spiritual life, and working together.

3. People in healthy congregations do well in these seven areas of their life and ministry: leadership; biblical and theological anchoring; Christian formation; worship; mission and outreach; welcome; and finance. Congregations that are both hopeful and healthy do better in these areas than either hopeful or healthy congregations.

4. Denominational leaders are very optimistic about the healthiness of their congregations. They are also very hopeful about their congregations. Pastors of hopeful, healthy, and both hopeful and healthy congregations believe their congregations do well in both overall hope and health. Congregations that are both hopeful and healthy have considerably higher

healthiness ratings than those for hopeful or healthy congregations. Being both hopeful and healthy matters!

5. People in healthy congregations do well in how they create community, communicate, treat one another, and work together. They also do well on all twenty-four marks of relational health. This includes six for community (build relationships, affirm and support one another, trust one another, show empathy, practice forgiveness, and bridge cultures); six for communication (engage conflict, listen to one another, find common ground, use technology, express appreciation, and exercise curiosity); six for character (do justice, show kindness, practice humility, feel compassion, demonstrate love, and promote peace); and six for collaboration (strategize and vision; discern and make decisions; be open to change; be agile organizationally; engage members' spiritual gifts; and partner and work collaboratively). These congregations are especially adept at these nine markers of relational health: building relationships, showing empathy, finding common ground, expressing appreciation, showing kindness, feeling compassion, demonstrating love, partnering, and discerning and making decisions. However, they are least adept at these six: practicing forgiveness, bridging cultures, engaging conflict, doing justice, being agile organizationally, and strategizing and visioning.

6. Hopeful and healthy congregations are both hopeful and healthy. While congregations identified as both hopeful and healthy are indeed both hopeful and healthy, they are considerably more healthy than hopeful.

5

Where Do We Go from Here?
Guidelines for Creating Hopeful and Healthy Congregations

AFTER LEARNING ABOUT SEVEN guidelines for making hope happen in chapter 1, examining eighteen models for creating healthy congregations in chapter 2, introducing a new way to understand signs of healthy congregations (a 4 C's relational perspective with its fresh signs of health) in chapter 3, and testing the validity and usefulness of this new approach along with our other signs of hope and health, it is time to take stock of where we go from here. Now, in chapter 5, here are six guidelines for creating hopeful and healthy futures for mainline churches that emerge from the results of this study.

Where Do We Go from Here?

GUIDELINES FOR CREATING HOPEFUL AND HEALTHY CONGREGATIONS

1. How congregations think about hope matters—we cannot live without hope.

A biblical understanding of hope is a good place to begin. Christian hope waits patiently and confidently for the unfolding of God's gift of salvation accomplished in Christ. God-centered faith creates an expectation about the future, trust, and the patience of waiting. This confidence has an active dimension comparable to making hope happen. Patience and persistence are involved. In other words, we may act with boldness as we live into God's future that awaits us.

Next, in our Christian tradition, we must remember that there can be no hope without truth being told, especially about global changes and challenges facing our world. In fact, the church's future is connected to mission and sustained by hope. In particular, that future, anchored in Good Friday and Easter, connects hope in Jesus with human suffering, freedom, and liberation. In short, ours is an active, living faith and hope with benefits, as Isa 40:31 makes clear: "But those who hope in the LORD will renew their strength. They will soar on wings like eagles; they will run and not grow weary, they will walk and not be faint."

Indeed, we cannot live without hope. This reality is a good reminder for pastors and congregations who are not optimistic about the future of their congregations—particularly when they are unwilling to change and me-focused. It gives them a rationale for making an attitude adjustment and a basis to renew their hope. It grounds hope in Jesus and makes hope realistic. And it spurs us to live out our faith in actions that demonstrate and partner with God's loving-kindness and justice for all who are needy and oppressed.

Hope is also a way of thinking that views hope as a choice we make and can learn. This reality leads to our second guideline.

2. Congregations can create the future they want for themselves by making hope happen.

For congregations, hope requires effort to set and pursue goals, including finding pathways around obstacles that stand in their way. Hope is goal-directed and requires willpower and waypower, and results of our research project identify how mainline congregations may do so. They make hope happen by setting and meeting their goals, energetically pursuing their goals, and solving problems even when people get discouraged. We also learned that people in both hopeful and healthy congregations are better at these three hopeful activities than people in either hopeful or healthy congregations. So, what are the takeaways from these findings?

First, when congregations wonder what they can do to make hope happen, they can realize that they need both the will and the way. Second, they can aspire to become both hopeful and healthy congregations. It is clear from our research that a way to do so centers on their leadership, spiritual life, outreach and mission-focus, willingness to change, and working together. Our research also underscores creating vitality from biblical and theological anchoring, Christian formation, being welcoming, financial stability, and Spirit-inspired and thought-provoking worship. Rare will be congregations that do all these activities exceptionally well, but neither need they be done poorly. Aim for doing them well or fairly well over time.

Here's a comment from a Gen Zer that illustrates the impact a hopeful and healthy congregation can make: "Hope seems to thrive when (1) you actually believe in the outcome and (2) when our purpose is kindness and love to all. When I first came here I had a very low belief in God due to my past experiences. Through acceptance and kindness, I began to build hope that even though life has gone wrong, if I continue to keep this congregation by my side Christ's love will continue to grow and prosper making life less of a battle." This same Gen Zer goes on to express ways a visitor might experience Spirit-filled worship: "A visitor may be used to other churches where they use the Word of God against you and hypocritize kindness and joy. You come here as you are, and we don't plane over who you are. The Spirit makes us comfortable where we are in our walk with Christ. We compare life to the Word and what's acceptable for our times leaving with thoughts to live our faith after the worship service."

The pastor of this 23-member congregation prepares the order of worship to flow and be inspiring. She crafts a new message with current events each Sunday. She also makes the space inviting with creative art installations to enhance the church calendar. For example, a blessing bowl painted by a famous Russian artist before leaving the country is a thing of beauty—and they no longer have to pass the offering plate. She also comments, "'Inclusive and affirming' in our mission statement sets the tone for members and guests to feel safe. We have at least three members who are Gen Z. We listen to them, validating their ideas and implementing them. At least two other members in the congregation are gay. This radical welcome is evident when guests step in the door not because we have pride flags but because the message is consistent from pulpit to fellowship." The radical intergenerational welcoming of this congregation exemplifies what an Alban at Duke Divinity School article suggests: "Doing intergenerational ministry well requires that those with power and positions, who today are often among the Greatest Generation and the boomers, practice radical hospitality to make room for the voices and visions that are not being heard or acknowledged. Also, younger disciples would do well to listen and learn from folks who've made incredible sacrifices to support our institutions."[1]

3. *It's all about relationships.*

Our relationships with one another in the church matter! From a relational perspective, signs of health in the church are evident in the 4 C's: community, communication, character, and collaboration. Community has to do with ways we share with one another to create Christian community; communication with ways

---

1. See Rivers, "Intergenerational Ministry Is Countercultural," para. 4.

Signs of Hope and Health in Mainline Churches

we interact with one another; character with ways we treat one another; and collaboration with ways we work with one another. Mainline denominational leaders, pastors, and congregations looking for marks of healthy congregations may concentrate on twenty-four specific signs of relational health.

They may create Christian community by doing these six activities well:

- Building relationships
- Affirming and supporting
- Experiencing trust
- Showing empathy
- Practicing forgiveness
- Bridging cultures

They may interact with one another well by enacting these six signs of healthy communication:

- Engaging conflict
- Listening attentively
- Finding common ground
- Technological savvy
- Expressing appreciation
- Exercising curiosity

They may treat one another well by embodying these six marks of healthy Christian character and behavior:

- Doing justice
- Showing kindness
- Practicing humility
- Feeling compassion
- Demonstrating love
- Promoting peace

Where Do We Go from Here?

Finally, they may work together well by collaborating in these six ways:

- Strategizing and visioning
- Discerning and decision-making
- Openness to change
- Organizational agility
- Engagement of spiritual gifts
- Partnering

Of these twenty-four areas of relational health, people in hopeful and healthy congregations seem to do especially well in these nine: building relationships, showing empathy, finding common ground, expressing appreciation, showing kindness, feeling compassion, demonstrating love, partnering, and discerning and making decisions. Congregations are encouraged to be vigilant about and even strengthen these areas of their relational life. Six areas that might warrant special attention include practicing forgiveness, bridging cultures, engaging conflict, doing justice, being agile organizationally, and strategizing and visioning.[2]

Here are comments from members of a hopeful and healthy small congregation that illustrate some of the ways these 4 C's are present in their congregation's life and ministry:

> "We limit hypocrisy and allow for troubles to be spoken aloud rather than hidden and dismissed, creating an environment that is very welcoming."

> "When we came here as a visitor, we were welcomed by kindness, humility, peace, and love."

> "Everyone here has been through different paths, some from different cultures, and other backgrounds but we are very inclusive."

---

2. For a synopsis of each of these twenty-four areas, including summaries of the latest relational and social science empirical research, see chapter 3.

"I have not seen hidden agendas! This is very rewarding to see and be a part of."

"Working together and sharing responsibility really helps the vitalization of our church. It allows everyone to know that it can be anyone's calling if you have the hope and knowledge that it's in God's hands. We bounce ideas that can collectively help because each person is very intelligent and thinks in their own way."

4. Create healthy congregations by doing seven activities well.

People in healthy congregations do well in leading effectively; anchoring their lives and ministries biblically and theologically; providing Christian formation; providing Spirit-inspired and thought-provoking worship; engaging in mission and outreach activities; welcoming new people; and achieving financial stability. Congregations that are both hopeful and healthy do better in these seven activities than either hopeful or healthy congregations. As we'll see in the next guideline, apparently being both healthy and hopeful seems to matter.

One way a hopeful and healthy 1300-member congregation expresses its welcome to new people is with this "About" statement on its website: "We welcome all those who are seeking a deeper relationship with God, a life patterned on the ways Jesus taught and lived, and an opportunity to make a difference for good in the world. We are an Open and Affirming congregation of the United Church of Christ." It then posts this expanded, multicolor, spacious "Statement of Welcome and Inclusion:"[3]

> We strive to be people of extravagant welcome. We affirm that all people are created in the image of God, and we celebrate the diversity of God's creation.
>
> As we seek to become faithful disciples of Jesus Christ and endeavor to live out our shared mission—Growing People to Serve God and Others—we respect and gladly

3. See Avon Lake United Church of Christ, "Statement of Welcome."

receive persons of every race, ethnicity, nationality, gender, gender identity and expression, sexual orientation, mental and physical ability, age, socioeconomic status, marital standing and family structure, and religious background.

We believe that our political differences can be a source of strength, as together we practice civil discourse.

We welcome those who are seekers, those who aren't sure what they believe, all who come in a spirit of openness and mutual respect.

We affirm that the Holy Spirit gathers us as a congregation in which all people are invited to participate in the life, leadership, ministry, fellowship, worship, sacraments, responsibilities, blessings, concerns, and joys of our community of faith. We hope and pray that by establishing and embodying this covenant of inclusion, we might fully follow Christ's commandment to love God and neighbor and be a safe place where love abounds.

This congregation also considers mission as part of its DNA. As they are in service to others, they find themselves growing spiritually and experiencing a deeper sense of joy and purpose. They express their focus on mission with food drives, special collections to support those in need, affiliations with several mission organizations, and offers of financial support. Hands-on volunteering opportunities with community partner agencies include drug and alcohol addiction recovery housing services, a domestic violence services center, and provision of health resources for mothers.

5. *Being both hopeful and healthy matters.*

As we saw earlier, congregations that are both hopeful and healthy are better at our three hopeful activities than either hopeful or healthy congregations. Moreover, as we've just noted, congregations that are both hopeful and healthy do better on our seven activities of healthy congregations than either hopeful or healthy congregations.

Furthermore, denominational leaders are very optimistic about the healthiness of their congregations. They are also very hopeful about their congregations. Pastors of hopeful, healthy, and both hopeful and healthy congregations believe their congregations do well in both overall hope and health. Significantly, congregations that are both hopeful and healthy have considerably higher healthiness ratings than those for hopeful or healthy congregations.

Finally, hopeful and healthy congregations are both hopeful and healthy. Moreover, congregations that are both hopeful and healthy are considerably more healthy than hopeful.

Indeed, it is clear that being both hopeful and healthy matters! For hopeful congregations and healthy congregations aspiring to be both hopeful and healthy, this study identifies a path to hope and health. In general, as we saw earlier, it is clear that a way to become hopeful and healthy centers on leadership, spiritual life, mission and outreach focus, willingness to change, and working together.

More specifically, hopeful congregations that would like to become more healthy congregations may seek to strengthen the seven areas of their lives and ministries that characterize healthy congregations: their leadership; biblical and theological anchoring; Christian formation; worship; mission and outreach; welcome; and financial stability. Surely they must be realistic in their expectations to enhance these activities, perhaps by drawing on their hopeful patience and persistence and the three activities that make hope happen: setting and meeting goals, energetically pursuing goals, and solving problems when they get discouraged.

Finally, healthy congregations that aspire to become more hopeful can practice hopeful patience and persistence and apply their three hopeful activities to the seven healthy activities they already do well.

A midsized congregation enhanced its hopefulness and health by having a strategic planning process beginning in 2018.

They created a five-year strategic plan with specific and measurable goals to guide their work in 2019–24. Rather than being a strategic plan that sat in a three-ring binder on a shelf, they made big banners and hung them in their fellowship hall. They also included the information at the top of every committee meeting agenda. This gave them purpose and direction, which helped to nurture hope in the face of changes and even conflicts. As they proceeded through COVID, they were able to refer back to their strategic plan which allowed them to stay focused, remember where they came from and where they were going, and continue to feel hopeful about their future. These practices got them through the COVID changes and allowed them to thrive.

6. Keep perspective—take care with generalization, representation, prescription, and causation.

It is important to keep in mind that the percentages, recurring themes, and activity ratings of hopeful and healthy churches reported in this study are based on perspectives of mainline denominational leaders and pastors who chose to respond. Care should be taken not to *generalize* from this study's conclusions to all churches, denominational leaders, or pastors. Moreover, perspectives of laypersons are not included. Would conclusions differ if more denominational leaders and pastors responded or had laypersons been included? The answer to this question is unknown. Even though respondents were assured of anonymity and confidentiality, perhaps some denominational leaders or pastors were reluctant to respond because they felt it is too risky to answer questions about the hopefulness and health of their congregations. Some may have been less hopeful and healthy than they wished to disclose. Others may simply have been questionnaire-response-adverse. Many people, me included, don't complete surveys as a rule. Then, too, whereas I was dependent upon and needed their participation, some denominational leaders or pastors may not be interested in this topic or identify as stakeholders in a study by an unknown researcher or one not connected to a research institution. Nonetheless, in spite of these potential limitations, clear and striking percentages, recurring themes, and activity ratings emerged from questionnaire respondents. It is worth noting that when I expanded the initial pool of denominational leaders from 250 to 500, only one change in recurring themes emerged: spiritual life was added to the list. Results for percentages and activity ratings characteristic of hopeful and healthy congregations remained essentially the same.

Another matter on which to keep perspective is the three marks of hopeful congregations, seven activities of healthy churches, 4 C's, and twenty-four characteristics of relational health selected for this study are not the only ones to consider. They may not be *representative* of all hopeful or healthy congregations. In other words, there are surely other characteristics of hopeful and healthy congregations. As one denominational leader put it, "Healthy congregations are not all healthy in the same way." Moreover, while signs of concern or disappointment are identified, this study does not explore activities characteristic of hopeless or less hopeful churches in any detail. What this study does confirm is that hopeful congregations in this study do set and meet goals, energetically pursue goals, and solve problems along the way. Likewise, hopeful and healthy congregations in this study did in fact do well or fairly well on all seven activities explored in this study, and healthy congregations in this study do well or fairly well on all twenty-four marks of community, communication, character, and collaboration.

Next, it is important to account for the distinction between *prescription* and description. Both are present in this book. For example, guidelines for making hope happen are prescribed in chapter 1, and guidelines for creating hopeful and healthy congregations are prescribed in this chapter. However, chapters 2, 3, and 4 focus more on "whats" than "hows." They identify and describe *what* signs of hope and health are characteristic of mainline churches. Striking recurring themes and key activities of hope and health are identified and illustrated. However, this book does not prescribe *how* to become mission-focused or provide such activities as Christian formation and Spirit-inspired, thought-provoking worship, and while it does address how to create community, communication, character, and collaboration, it does not prescribe how to live into the twenty-four ways of doing so.

Finally, it is important to be aware that *causation* is not assured. As just mentioned, much of this study is more descriptive than prescriptive. Our three hopeful activities, seven healthy activities, 4 C's, and twenty-four relational behaviors do not guarantee congregational hope and health. They are characteristics that describe congregations in this study, and as such are worthy candidates to consider for creating hopeful and healthy congregations. However, they are not guarantees of success nor the only ways to create hopeful and healthy churches.

SUMMARY

Six guidelines for creating hopeful and healthy churches are presented in chapter 5. We learned that while congregations need hope to survive and thrive, they can make hope happen. Hope is goal-directed and includes both willpower and waypower. Being both hopeful and healthy matters—hopeful and healthy congregations are both hopeful and healthy. Practical ways to make hope happen, along with recurring themes and activities identified with hopeful and healthy congregations, are verified as bona fide candidates for creating hopeful and healthy congregations. Along with leadership and practices, relationships in the church matter. Community, communication, character, and collaboration are shown to affect relational health in our congregations, and twenty-four practices for doing so are prescribed and confirmed. Care must be taken with the results of this study not to overgeneralize, ignore alternate signs of hope and health, mistake prescriptions for description, or attribute causality where none may exist.

In conclusion, as promised at the beginning of this book, heretofore unknown assessments and surprising findings about the hope and health of twenty-first-century mainline churches from the perspectives of their denominational leaders and pastors are featured. It does indeed seem timely and warranted to replace lament over problems facing mainline churches with the aspirations of hope and possibilities of health revealed in this study.

PRACTICAL APPLICATIONS

1. Identify the most prominent signs of hope and health in twenty-first-century mainline churches. How about in your congregation?

2. What hopeful and healthy activities are most important in twenty-first-century mainline churches? How about in your congregation?

3. How well does your congregation do on the hopeful and healthy activities identified in this study? What other activities do you think are important, if any?

4. What are the ways your congregation creates Christian community? What might enhance its capacity to do so? Consider the six ways to create community identified in this study.

5. What are healthy and unhealthy ways people in your congregation communicate with one another? What might improve the way people interact with one another? Consider the six ways identified in this study.

6. What are healthy and unhealthy ways people in your congregation treat one another? What are better ways to better relationships? Consider the six character strengths identified in this study.

7. What are healthy and unhealthy ways people in your congregation work with one another? What would improve the way they collaborate? Consider the six ways to collaborate identified in this study.

8. What are other signs of relational health, if any? What are other practices or behaviors to consider, if any? What are

other ways to create community, communicate, treat one another, and collaborate, if any?

About the Author

THOMAS G. KIRKPATRICK IS an educator, pastor, trainer, writer, and consultant with specialties in interpersonal communication, small group ministries, and conflict management. He is the author of the Roman and Littlefield (Alban) publications *Communication in the Church: A Handbook for Healthier Relationships* and *Small Groups in the Church: A Handbook for Creating Community*, along with the Wipf & Stock publication *Better Ways to Better Relationships in the Church: Guidelines for Practicing Humility, Experiencing Empathy, Feeling Compassion, Showing Kindness, Expressing Appreciation, and Doing Justice*. He has been an adjunct professor at the University of Dubuque Theological Seminary, pastor of Westminster United Presbyterian Church, Galena, Illinois, and associate pastor of Little Church on the Prairie Presbyterian Church, Lakewood, Washington. Previously, he was associate professor of speech communication at Whitworth University in Spokane, Washington. He has also served as a campus minister and a program director of camps and conferences. He received his MA and PhD from the University of Washington, DMin from San Francisco Theological Seminary, MDiv from Fuller Theological Seminary, and BMusEd from the University of Oregon. He lives with his wife, also a PCUSA minister, in Maple Valley, Washington, and his four children live in Portland, Oregon; Harrisburg, Oregon; La Crosse, Wisconsin; and Snohomish, Washington.

You can reach him at his website, www.tomkirkpatrick.org.

Appendix 1

Research Design

Hypothesis 1: Hopeful congregations will do well in finding ways to set and meet their goals, energetically pursue their goals, and solve problems even when people get discouraged.

Psychologist C. R. Snyder created a six-item Adult State Hope Scale using the following statements:[1]

- If I should find myself in a jam, I could think of many ways to get out of it.
- At the present time, I am energetically pursuing my goals.
- There are lots of ways around any problem that I am facing now.
- Right now, I see myself as being pretty successful.
- I can think of many ways to reach my current goals.
- At this time, I am meeting the goals that I have set for myself.

1. See Snyder, *Psychology of Hope*, 321–35.

Appendix 1

To test hypothesis 1, these three questions were created for denominational leaders in six mainline churches:

- How well do hopeful congregations in your region set and meet their goals?
- How well do hopeful congregations in your region energetically pursue their goals?
- How well do hopeful congregations in your region find ways to solve problems even when people get discouraged?

Similar questions were created for pastors.

Hypothesis 2: Both denominational leaders and pastors will provide fresh signs of hope and signs of health in mainline churches.

These four inquiries were created to identify signs of hope, signs of concern or disappointment, conditions in which hope thrives, and signs of a healthy congregation:

- Reflecting on congregations in your region for which you are most hopeful, list one or two signs of hope that make your heart sing.
- Reflecting on congregations in your region for which you are least hopeful, list one or two signs of concern or disappointment that make your heart ache.
- In thinking about the most hopeful congregations in your region, list one or two of the conditions in which it seems hope thrives.
- Many church leaders and members would like their congregations to be vital, lively, thriving, or flourishing. List one or two signs of a healthy congregation.

A similar set of questions was created for pastors.

Research Design

Hypothesis 3: Healthy congregations do well in their leadership, biblical and theological anchoring, Christian formation, worship, mission and outreach, welcome, and finances.

Drawn from the eighteen conceptions of healthy congregations reviewed in chapter 2, baseline questions were created to identify signs of a healthy congregation, assess congregational health, and assess how well healthy congregations do in these seven major areas of their life and ministry: leadership, biblical and theological anchoring, Christian formation, worship, mission and outreach, welcome, and finances. To test hypothesis 3, these eight questions were created for denominational leaders:

- How do you rate the overall health of congregations in your region?[2]
- How do you rate the overall effectiveness of leaders in healthy congregations in your region?
- How well do healthy congregations in your region anchor their lives and ministries biblically and theologically?
- How well do healthy congregations in your region provide Christian formation?
- How well do healthy congregations in your region provide Spirit-inspired, thought-provoking worship?
- How well do healthy congregations in your region engage in mission and outreach?
- How well do healthy congregations in your region welcome new people?

---

2. Respondents were asked to rate each item using a scale of 1 to 6 where "1" is "very poor" or "not well" and "6" is "excellent" or "very well." A six-point Likert scale was used rather than the more common five- or seven-point scale so as to avoid the hard-to-interpret middle rating ("3" or "4"). For example, are respondents uncertain about how to respond or ambivalent rather than genuinely in the middle? Also, as we'll see later, results may be easily grouped for interpretative purposes.

- How well do healthy congregations in your region achieve financial stability?

A similar set of questions was created for pastors.

Hypothesis 4: People in hopeful and healthy congregations do well in how they create Christian community, communicate with one another, treat one another, and work with one another.

Hypothesis 4 is derived from the 4 C's relational perspective about healthy congregations presented in chapter 3.

To test hypothesis 4, these four questions were created for denominational leaders:

- How well do people in healthy congregations in your region create Christian community?
- How well do people in healthy congregations in your region communicate with one another?
- How well do people in healthy congregations in your region treat one another?
- How well do people in healthy congregations in your region work with one another?

Similar questions were created for pastors.

Hypothesis 5: Denominational leaders will report that around one-third of congregations in their region are healthy.

Hypothesis 5 is based on Faith Communities Today's 2020 research survey of over fifteen thousand religious communities from eighty different denominations and faith traditions, 20 percent of whom are mainline Protestant congregations, wherein about one-third of congregations surveyed reported that they are spiritually vital and alive. It should be noted that their definition of vitality

Research Design

is somewhat different from our notion of congregational health. Moreover, since 80 percent of denominations in their survey are other than mainline Protestant, including 71 percent from Evangelical Protestant congregations, care must be taken when comparing results from our mainline churches.

It should also be noted that this hypothesis does not include a prediction for the proportion of congregations that denominational leaders identify as hopeful. However, our questionnaire results will provide this information from our respondents.

Denominational leaders were asked to assess the overall health of churches in their regions using this question:

- How do you rate the overall health of congregations in your region?

In addition, these two optional questions were created to learn how hopeful denominational leaders are about churches in their regions and how healthy churches are in their regions:

- For what percent of congregations in your region are you hopeful? (optional)
- What percent of congregations in your region are healthy? (optional)

Google Forms questionnaires were sent to five hundred denominational leaders in six mainline churches for which I had email addresses (see appendix 2): all 134 Presbyterian Church (USA) executive presbyters, 144 of 319 United Methodist Church district superintendents, all 90 Episcopal Church bishops, all 65 Evangelical Lutheran Church in America bishops, all 34 United Church of Christ conference ministers, and all 33 American Baptist Churches executive ministers.[3]

---

3. For a sample Signs of Hope and Health Questionnaire sent to denominational leaders, see this link: https://forms.gle/LF66BJXJuSZGcUFj7.

Appendix 1

Hypothesis 6: People in hopeful and healthy congregations do well in experiencing sets of six ways they create Christian community, communicate with one another, treat one another, and work with one another.

To test this hypothesis, denominational leaders were asked to identify the most hopeful and healthy churches in their regions using these two optional inquiries:

- Please list one or two of the most hopeful churches in your region to contact for further information. (optional)
- Please list one or two of the most healthy churches in your region to contact for further information. (optional)

Follow-up questionnaires to pastors of these hopeful and healthy churches were designed to gain their perspective on signs of hope and health and to obtain in-depth information about the sets of six ways healthy congregations create Christian community, communicate with one another, treat one another, and work with one another.

In a follow-up seventeen-item questionnaire to pastors of healthy congregations identified by denominational leaders, the signs of health question from hypothesis 2 and the twelve questions used in hypotheses 3 and 4 were included, as were a question about how hopeful pastors are about their congregation and the 3 questions about hope used in hypothesis 1. To test hypothesis 6, an additional set of six sub-questions crafted to assess specific ways people in healthy congregations create Christian community, communicate, treat one another, and work together was included as follows:

- How well do people in your congregation create Christian community in these six ways: build relationships, affirm and support one another, trust one another, show empathy, practice forgiveness, and bridge cultures?
- How well do people in your congregation communicate with one another in these six ways: engage conflict, listen to one

another, find common ground, use technology, express appreciation, and exercise curiosity?

- How well do people in your congregation treat one another in these six ways: do justice, show kindness, practice humility, feel compassion, demonstrate love, and promote peace?

- How well do people in your congregation work with one another in these six ways: strategize and vision, discern and make decisions, be open to change, be agile organizationally, engage members' spiritual gifts, and partner and work collaboratively?

Hypothesis 7: Hopeful congregations also tend to be healthy congregations and vice versa.

In a follow-up nineteen-item questionnaire to pastors of congregations for which denominational leaders are most hopeful, the same twelve questions created for denominational leaders about healthy congregations were used to explore whether hopeful congregations are also healthy congregations. Seven questions geared specifically to signs of hopeful congregations were also included, one asking how hopeful pastors are about their congregation, the three questions about hope from hypothesis 3, and the three questions from hypothesis 1.

Likewise, in the follow-up questionnaire to pastors of congregations that denominational leaders identified as most healthy, the four questions about hope were used to explore whether healthy congregations are also hopeful congregations.

Since denominational leaders also identified congregations for which they are most hopeful and that are most healthy, a twenty-item questionnaire combining the seven questions about hope and thirteen questions about health, including the six sets of additional sub-questions, was sent to pastors of these churches to explore whether these churches do well on both hopeful and healthy measures.

Appendix 1

Three Google Forms questionnaires were sent to 104 pastors of congregations identified by denominational leaders and for which I had email addresses (see appendix 2): one to 39 pastors of hopeful congregations, another to 41 pastors of healthy congregations, and the third to 24 pastors of both hopeful and healthy congregations.[4] In addition, a pretest trial questionnaire was sent to 4 pastors of healthy congregations in my presbytery, without including the four questions about hope.

---

4. For a sample Signs of Hope and Health Questionnaire sent to pastors of hopeful and health churches, see this link: https://forms.gle/vs5YhQukWp79ZjRK8

Appendix 2

Emails to Denominational Leaders

EMAILS WERE SENT TO five hundred denominational leaders inviting them to submit questionnaire responses using a Google Form link. Follow-up reminder emails extending the response deadline were also sent. Here's a sample of the initial email.

> Dear Denominational Leaders,
> I am researching signs of hope and health in mainline congregations. I need your help.
> Your perspective as a denominational leader is critical to this project. I am reaching out to nearly 500 of your colleagues in six mainline denominations: ELCA, United Methodist, PCUSA, UCC, American Baptist, and the Episcopal Church.
> It should take 15–20 minutes to complete a 23-item questionnaire. Your participation will be much appreciated, and I thank you in advance for your responses.
> Here's the URL link to complete the questionnaire:
> [Google Forms questionnaire link]
> *The deadline for responses is Monday, June 5, 2023.* I will handle your responses with confidentiality and anonymity.

Appendix 2

I expect to publish the results of this research and writing project as a companion volume to my previous publications, one on small groups in the church (1995), another on communication in the church (2016), and the third on better ways to better relationships in the church (2021). For more information about myself and these publications, check out my website, https://tom-kirkpatrick.org.

Grateful to partner in ministry,
Rev. Tom Kirkpatrick, Ph.D.
Email: tomgkirkpatrick@comcast.net
Cell: 253.569.0644

And here is a sample of the follow-up email:

Hi Again,

Thank you to those who have completed my questionnaire. Your responses are revealing some very striking signs of hope and health in mainline denominations.

Some denominational leaders have been on vacation, study leave, or sabbatical. So, *I've extended the deadline for responses to Thursday, June 15, 2023.*

Your participation is critical to the completion of this project. I hope this extra time gives more of you an opportunity to respond (see questionnaire link below).

Rev. Tom Kirkpatrick, Ph.D.

EMAILS TO PASTORS

Emails were sent to 104 pastors inviting them to submit questionnaire responses using a Google Form link, one to pastors of hopeful churches, one to pastors of healthy churches, and one to pastors of both hopeful and healthy churches. Follow-up reminder emails extending the initial deadline were also sent. Here's a sample of the initial email.

Dear Pastor,

I am researching signs of hope and health in mainline churches. I need your help.

Your perspective as pastor is critical to this project. I am reaching out to pastors of hopeful and healthy

Emails to Denominational Leaders

congregations. I've been referred to your congregation from a Signs of Hope and Health Questionnaire I sent to 500 denominational leaders in six mainline denominations: PCUSA, ELCA, UCC, United Methodist, American Baptist, and the Episcopal Church.

It should take around 20 minutes to complete a 20-item questionnaire. Your participation will be much appreciated, and I thank you in advance for your responses.

The deadline for responses is August 7, 2023. I will handle your responses with confidentiality and anonymity.

Here is the URL link to complete the questionnaire: [Google Forms questionnaire link]

I expect to publish the results of this research and writing project in a book currently titled *Signs of Hope and Health in Mainline Churches*. It will be a companion volume to my previous publications, one on small groups in the church (1995), another on communication in the church (2016), and the third on better ways to better relationships in the church (2021). If you'd like more information about myself or these publications, check out my website, https://tomkirkpatrick.org.

With gratitude,
Rev. Tom Kirkpatrick, Ph.D.

And here is a sample of the follow-up email.

Hi Again,

Initial questionnaire responses reveal some very striking signs of hope and health in mainline churches.

However, since some pastors have been on vacation, study leave, or sabbatical, I've extended the deadline for responses. *The deadline for responses is now August 18, 2023.*

Your participation in this research project will be very much appreciated. I hope this extra time gives more of you an opportunity to respond (see questionnaire link below).

With gratitude,
Tom Kirkpatrick

Appendix 3

Denominational Leader Recurring Themes

For what are you most hopeful?

1. Working Together (53%)[1] **
2. Mission-Focused (40%)**
3. Outreach (39%)*
4. Willing to Change (35%)*
5. Spiritual Life (14%)

For what are you least hopeful?

1. Unwilling to Change (75%) ***
2. Me-Focused (60%) ***
3. Weak Leadership (33%)
4. Spiritual Life (16%)

1. Percent of times cited by fifty-seven respondents.

Denominational Leader Recurring Themes

Conditions in which hope thrives

1. Strong Leadership (49%) **
2. Spiritual Life (39%)*
3. Mission-Focused (37%)*
4. Organization (32%)
5. Willing to Change (25%)

Signs of healthy congregations

1. Spiritual Life (60%) ***
2a. Mission-Focused (39%)*
2b. Strong Leadership (39%)*
4. Outreach (26%)
5. Willing to Change (25%)

*** Striking responses
** Notable responses
* Borderline responses

Appendix 4

Pastor Recurring Themes

For what are you most hopeful?

1. Mission-Focused (70%)[1] ***
2. Outreach (60%) ***
3. Working Together (50%) **
4. Willing to Change (30%)

For what are you least hopeful?

1. Unwilling to Change (50%)[2] **
2. Me-Focused (40%)**
3. Working Together (20%)
4. Spiritual Life (20%)

---

1. Percent of times cited by ten respondents (four hopeful and six both hopeful and healthy).

2. Percent of times cited by ten respondents (four hopeful and six both hopeful and healthy).

Pastor Recurring Themes

Conditions in which hope thrives

1. Spiritual Life (60%)[3] ***
2. Mission-Focused (40%)**
3. Working Together (30%)
4. Willing to Change (10%)

Signs of healthy congregations

1. Spiritual Life (89%)[4] ***
2. Mission-Focused (44%)**
3. Working Together (39%)*
4. Outreach (17%)

*** Striking responses
** Notable responses
* Borderline responses

---

3. Percent of times cited by 10 respondents (4 hopeful and 6 both hopeful and healthy)

4. Percent of times cited by 18 respondents (12 healthy and 6 both hopeful and healthy)

Appendix 5

Denominational Leader Questionnaire Responses

HOPEFUL CONGREGATIONS

Overall*

Very hopeful	22%
Hopeful	59%
Not very hopeful	14%
Other	5%

Activities**

Pursue goals	4.9
Set and meet goals	4.9
Solve problems	4.7

DENOMINATIONAL LEADER QUESTIONNAIRE RESPONSES

HEALTHY CONGREGATIONS

*Overall**

Very healthy	18%
Healthy	50%
Not very healthy	21%
Other	11%

*Activities*****

Overall health	3.5
Mission and outreach	5.2
Leadership	5.1
Biblical and theological anchoring	5.1
Worship	4.8
Welcoming	4.7
Christian formation	4.6
Financial stability	4.5

*4 C's*****

Character	4.9
Community	4.9
Collaboration	4.5
Communication	4.3

* Reports percentage of responses rated 75 percent to 100 percent (very hopeful), 50 percent (hopeful), 0 percent to 25 percent (not very hopeful), or not rated (other). Respondents: 56

** Reports position on a scale between 1 and 6 where 1 is "not well" or "very poor" and 6 is "very well" or "excellent." Respondents: 57.

Appendix 6

Pastor Questionnaires Responses

Respondents	Hope (4)	Health (12)	Both (6)	Total (22)
Overall hope	4.5*	4.9	4.7	4.8
Activities				
Solve problems	4.8	4.9	5.5	5.0
Pursue goals	4.5	4.7	5.3	4.7
Set and meet goals	4.5	4.3	5.2	4.6
Overall health	4.3	4.5	5.3	4.7
Activities				
Mission and outreach	5.5	4.8	6.0	5.3
Worship	5.0	5.3	5.5	5.3
Welcoming	5.5	5.0	4.8	5.0
Leadership	5.3	4.6	5.3	4.9
Financial stability	4.0	4.6	5.3	4.9
Biblical and theological anchoring	5.0	4.6	5.2	4.8
Christian formation	4.0	4.1	5.0	4.5

Pastor Questionnaires Responses

4 C's

Character	5.5	5.1	5.2	5.2
Collaboration	5.5	5.1	5.3	5.2
Community	5.0	4.6	5.2	4.8
Communication	4.8	4.2	4.8	4.5

* Denotes position on a scale between 1 and 6 where 1 is "not well" or "very poor" and 6 is "very well" or "excellent." Number of respondents: 22.

Appendix 7

4 C's Questionnaires Responses

Respondents	Health (12)	Health and Hope (6)	Combined (18)
Community	4.6*	5.2	4.8
Show empathy	5.2	5.7	5.4
Build relationships	4.7	5.5	5.0
Affirm and support	5.2	5.3	4.8
Experience trust	4.4	5.0	4.6
Practice forgiveness	4.3	4.7	4.4
Bridge cultures	4.0	4.2	4.1
Average	4.6	5.1	4.7

4 C's Questionnaires Responses

Communication	4.2	4.8	4.4
Find common ground	4.8	5.7	5.1
Express appreciation	4.9	5.3	5.0
Listen	4.5	5.3	4.8
Exercise curiosity	4.8	4.8	4.8
Use technology	4.6	4.8	4.7
Engage conflict	3.8	4.5	4.0
Average	*4.6*	*5.1*	*4.7*
Character	5.1	5.2	5.1
Show kindness	5.0	5.8	5.3
Demonstrate love	5.1	5.5	5.2
Feel compassion	5.1	5.2	5.1
Practice humility	4.7	5.0	4.8
Promote peace	4.7	4.8	4.7
Do justice	4.1	4.7	4.3
Average	*4.7*	*5.2*	*4.9*
Collaboration	5.1	5.3	5.2
Partner and work collaboratively	4.8	5.7	5.1
Discern and make decisions	4.8	5.5	5.0
Be open to change	4.7	4.7	4.7
Engage member's spiritual gifts	4.4	4.8	4.5
Be agile organizationally	4.3	4.7	4.4
Strategize and vision	4.3	4.3	4.3
Average	*4.6*	*5.0*	*4.7*

* Denotes position on a scale between 1 and 6 where 1 is "not well" or "very poor" and 6 is "very well" or "excellent."

Appendix 8

Case Study—Chapel by the Sea
Moclips/Pacific Beach, Washington

Mission Statement

Bringing God's Inclusive, Affirming, Welcoming Love to All as We Work for Justice and Peace

Visitor Comments

"I really liked the people, ambience and the warm hospitality offered."

"Chapel by the Sea is a non-judgmental, kind group with a very attentive pastor."

"CBTS has an inspired mission-focus, especially evident in the spiritual gift of hospitality."

"Best little church I know. When you visit you will be welcomed back as family! We shared a lite lunch after 10:30 worship and had time to feel 'known.' Love those folks."

Case Study—Chapel by the Sea

Social Media

- Facebook (488 followers)
- Instagram (835 posts and 333 followers)
- Twitter (39 followers)

Many varied photos and videos are posted featuring a bagpiper in worship, concerts, artworks, a civil rights movement display, the food bank, Earth Day, and "meet the pastor" and guest preacher videos. Tags include only "mainline church," "progressive," "open," "inclusive," "Presbyterian," and "Reformed."

Membership

Chapel by the Sea (CBTS) recently cleaned up its membership rolls. In the last five years, they went from fourteen members to thirty-four. However, some members moved away or, after COVID, did not return to church. CBTS now has a healthy, active membership of twenty-three members and over twenty in worship on Sundays. Since CBTS is in a recreational area, it also has many friends who are members in other congregations, visit now and then, and send donations either online or by mail.

It is remarkable that this small church was able to bring their pastor on full-time two years ago! A generous benefactor (non-member) made this possible. The theme of this year's stewardship letter is "We Walk by Faith."

Signs of Hope and Health
(Comments from Pastor and Leadership Team)

Change

> "The willingness to change was stated from the beginning of my ministry: 'pastor, whatever you want to do...within reason and accountability, of course.'"

Appendix 8

"We are open to change, incorporating newer Gen Z and Millennial ideas and desires into our congregation's life and ministry. Youth attendance helps a lot with our congregation because we understand a certain way that they don't."

Focus

"Our mission statement stands as an authentic description of the progressive church we aspire to be."

"Our congregation has always had a heart for the poor and feeding the hungry in our rural area. We've stepped up our help to local food banks both financially and helping out by being present to meet those who need help. We distribute Christmas meals in partnership with a community organization and are a distribution point for food boxes. A lunch program started by one of our members delivers sack lunches to kids at home in the summer and over holidays. We also offer a thanksgiving meal at the church."

"We became an Earth Care congregation because of concern over the climate crisis and a desire to be good stewards of the earth. We installed a tankless water heater. We signed up for Adopt-a-Highway and have a two-mile section that we patrol for litter. Our last event was on Earth Day and 12 people showed up to help. We want to make this more of a community outreach service project."

"We give money to those in need and help even those not in our congregation for no intention other than spreading love."

"We have a group working to help a prisoner transition to life outside of prison."

Working Together

"As a small church the leaders have to work collaboratively as a committee of the whole. Our leadership is still very pastor driven. We are working on leaders taking the initiative and leading worship which a few of them have done. Training liturgists has been a positive growth experience."

"Everyone here is involved in our leadership, none less than others and I think that is a staple in our success. Here it's not just about God's word and ways of teaching, it's also leading our own healthy version of Christ's way that we can understand and adapt."

"The leadership has noted that healthy boundaries and not shying away from conflict ultimately works for the betterment of all. Whether it's a member who is doing too much or saying no to a proposed Bible study because it does not align with our sense of mission, the leaders are learning to speak up, have direct conversations, set healthy boundaries, and hold each other accountable."

Spiritual Life

"Spiritual life is a core value and there is always a study or book club either online or in person each week."

"Prayer is fuel for the Holy Spirit and all action is predicated on this spiritual discipline. Each day during the COVID lockdown the pastor would go to the chapel to pray. Leaders recently asked if we could have a Prayer Box in addition to the huge white board, prayer list, and cards."

Appendix 8

Vital Congregations Initiative (VCI)

Background

Rev. Dr. Linda Flatley arrived at CBTS in September 2018 as Designated Pastor for Revitalization. A grant from Olympia Presbytery for $15,000 each year for two years was received to help bring an installed pastor to the area twenty-four hours a week. From day one, the mission was clear: *revitalization*. There was a time frame and sense of urgency: two years to return to a "pastor in residence" which they had not had in ten years. Pastor Linda was willing to live in the manse behind the chapel.

Pastor Linda's personal sense of call and experience contributed to being called to CBTS. She is a trained interim pastor, having studied family systems and participated in a Holy Cow mission study at her previous church—all of which was helpful at CBTS. Her husband had recently retired, and they were empty nesters. So, this gave her and her husband a sense of mission to see what God would do if they invested some time and resources.

Trusting God in personal and collective discernment that this was God's timing, Pastor Linda decided to move into the area. She knew that God always goes ahead to prepare the way. She knew CBTS had potential. Her plan was to offer retreats, and an elder thought they could make CBTS a wedding venue. The congregation's life and ministry is centered in divine worship and a mission to help the poor, for example by getting involved with food banks, providing school lunches, and donating clothing—all mission projects they had taken on in the past.

Preparation

In May 2019, Pastor Linda attended a VCI conference in Denver along with pastors from other VCI congregations in Olympia Presbytery. CBTS was part of the "first wave" of VCI churches after the denominational pilot program. The presbytery had also signed on to the VCI, so there was support from both the presbytery and

Case Study—Chapel by the Sea

the national church. This was not another "program." It was an "initiative."

The congregation was concerned about the cost. However, it seemed like a good fit and way forward: the pastor for revitalization was recommending a Vital Congregations Initiative. The session was on board. Pastor Linda often reminded session members that the VCI recommends to not focus on the 4 B's: But-we've-never-done-it-that-way-before, Building, Budget, and Bodies (note: she didn't want to offend anyone by using the VCI phrase, "B" for "butts in pews," so she changed it to Bodies—warm bodies in worship).

The VCI is a two-year commitment: year one "relational" and year two "incarnational." CBTS spent six months prior to the kick-off in preparation and prayer. After Pentecost in 2019, they spent another fifty days praying for their VCI. Pray. Pray. Pray. It was a huge learning curve for Pastor Linda—and this was pre-pandemic! The pastors of VCI churches in Olympia Presbytery became a cohort group and met monthly along with three Presbytery-appointed facilitators.

In January 2020, the VCI churches were commissioned at a Presbytery meeting. On February 9, 2020, Pastor Linda held a session retreat and invited their VCI facilitator, Rev. Dr. David Kegley, to meet with them. Pastor Linda remembers David asking the session, "So, you know a little about VCI?" He got blank stares. They were like deer caught in the headlights—or playing possum. In reality, some elders had not yet caught the vision or didn't fully understand the VCI. Like the disciples, right! Pastor Linda found the VCI a very pastor-driven initiative at the beginning and until she was able to get the session fully on board.

On February 23, 2020, CBTS held their opening celebration of VCI during worship with a special liturgy, candle lighting, and presentation of the "seven marks of vital congregations." Pastor Linda planned a seven-week sermon series along with VCI Bible studies immediately after each worship service using the VCI leaders guide. Well, we all know what happened in March 2020: everything shut down due to COVID-19.

APPENDIX 8

By March 8, 2020, CBTS was three sermons and Bible studies into the seven-week series when they closed their doors to in-person worship. They were all like deer caught in the headlights. What were they going to do now?

Like many congregations, Zoom became their new go-to communication tool and worship venue. *VCI was put on the backburner.*

The congregation's leaders and members had to learn to use new technologies and adapt to a new normal. If the core group (some in their eighties) had not done so, the VCI outcome might have been different. So, kudos to a "tiny but mighty congregation" for being willing and able to learn new ways of being the church!

CBTS slowly pivoted to Zoom worship and Pastor Linda initiated daily prayer in the chapel at noon. The VCI cohort continued to meet monthly via Zoom. These meetings gave pastors opportunity to vent their frustrations and to learn from each other. It soon became clear that CBTS was no longer time-driven as the VCI leader guide suggests. Their VCI experience became task-oriented, giving them the freedom to go at their own pace through a very difficult time of the pandemic.

March 2020–May 2021

While staying on-task and on-topic, CBTS was able to complete the following:

- The remaining four sermon series and Bible studies
- The neighborhood exegesis—adapted to fit the pandemic mitigation plan
- Telling the congregation's story after worship on Zoom
- The VCI survey—most people took it online
- Sharing survey results ("marks") with the congregation—giving some forward momentum
- Celebrating their "marks" on February 14, 2021—David Kegley joined the congregation for worship on Zoom

Case Study—Chapel by the Sea

May 2021–August 2021

On Mother's Day 2021, CBTS reopened to in-person worship, and they restarted the second year Bible study in June 2021. Pastor Linda preached from the Bible study texts for "Revitalizing the Seven Marks" in worship, providing context for the hour-long Bible study after worship. People stayed for the Bible studies, participated, and were engaged. During each study, they wrote their "Big Ideas" on large Post-it notes. They also had an intentional week of prayer.

At the end of the seven-week sermon series and Bible studies, the session met to discern which of three options to adopt:

- Reforming church—revitalizing the Seven Marks of Vital Congregations
- Clustering churches—revitalizing by clustering congregations into new communities of worship and ministry
- Reenvisioning church—revitalizing by grace and gratitude in the death and legacy of a congregation in witness to the resurrection

CBTS invited the presbytery's Transitional Executive Presbyter to be present for the session meeting at which it voted to *Reform CBTS*: "Once reformed[,] always being reformed according to the word of God in the power of the Spirit and in Jesus' name." On August 1, 2021, CBTS held an open house to celebrate their VCI experience.

Looking Ahead

At a session retreat in 2024, they will review CBTS's vitality and refocus their mission.

Appendix 9

Case Study—First Presbyterian Church
Hastings, Nebraska

Membership

462 active members, 201 affiliated friends

Website

https://fpchastings.org

Welcome

Our church is a warm and loving church, and we want you to feel comfortable and at liberty to call on us for anything you need. When you visit our church, you will find:

- A caring congregation that will gladly welcome you
- Preaching/teaching that is centered on the Word of God
- Ministries to meet the spiritual needs of every age

Case Study—First Presbyterian Church

Vision

Sharing the love of Christ from the heart of Hastings since 1873

Mission

Welcoming all
 Living the love of God and neighbor
 Seeking to transform ourselves, our community, and our world to be more Christ-like through service, worship, prayer, education, and fellowship

Social Media

- Facebook (1.3K followers)
- YouTube (165 subscribers, 512 videos)

Annual Report—January 28, 2024

State of the Church Address, January 29, 2023, Minutes:

> Pastor Greg reports that FPC continues to *grow and thrive* thanks to the efforts of the congregation and the staff. He is *appreciative* of everyone's continued giving, prayers, volunteers, creativity and dedication. *Highlights* include the addition of 11 new members (11 deaths), a 3 percent growth in attendance, and the creative in-person worship opportunities that included jazz and blue grass music as well as nine services in the park. Regarding *church viability*, one can sense a positive spirit and a deeper sense of engagement surrounding FPC. There is more volunteering both inside the church and within the greater community and one sees more children and youth participating in the many programs offered.

Appendix 9

Worship Service

April 21, 2024 (via Facebook link and worship bulletin download: https://www.facebook.com/fpchastings/videos/1585130445578606)

Hope-Centered Welcome: "We are a community of hope where you will always hear a message of hope proclaimed."

Coherence: The service is integrated around the Scriptures-and-worship theme, including call to worship, time with children, music, prayer of confession, sermon, etc.

Spirit-Filled, Thought-Provoking: Evident in welcome, children's choir, accompanist/organist, call to confession, sermon, offering invitation, benediction, blessing, and postlude.

Freshness: Apparent in call to worship, prayer of confession, affirmation of faith, sermon (including visual aids), and more.

Inviting: Evident in welcome, call to confession, offertory, prayers of people, benediction and blessing. Also evident in Facebook Live preservice announcements and in-service video prompts.

Inclusive and Skilled Worship Leaders: Includes head of staff, associate, organist, candlelighters, children's choir, and time with children.

Practical: Apparent in attractive and user-friendly bulletin; prelude and postlude offered as opportunities for worship with God and a time for prayer/meditation/reflection; silent confession focused with "question for contemplation"; time with children interactive using multiple ways of learning and takeaway application; practical applications in sermon, including example of Perico congregation of "help and hope" to bring the point home and learn from another culture.

Technological Savvy: Evident in Facebook video live streaming/TV broadcast, radio simulcast, and video-projected sermon points, hymns, etc.

Case Study—First Presbyterian Church

Signs of Hope and Health Questionnaire (Completed by Senior Pastor/Head of Staff Rev. Greg Allen-Pickett, July 25, 2023)

The congregation is both hopeful and healthy.

Signs of hope include church-wide commitment to mission, growth in numbers, and a positive spirit.

Signs of congregations that are not very hopeful include no outward focused mission projects and disengaged members.

Conditions in which hope thrives include serving the larger community outside the church's walls and music programs that connect people to one another and attract people outside the church's membership.

The congregation is doing "well" making hope happen by setting and meeting goals, energetically pursuing goals, and solving problems even when people get discouraged.

Signs of health include engagement in worship, music, and service and mission.

The overall effectiveness of leaders in the congregation is "very good."

The congregation is doing "very well" anchoring its life and ministry biblically and theologically, engaging in mission and outreach activities, and achieving financial stability; and doing "well" providing Christian formation, providing Spirit-inspired thought-provoking worship, and welcoming new people.

The congregation is doing "well" in creating Christian community. It is doing "very well" affirming and supporting one another; doing "well" building relationships and showing empathy; and doing "fairly well" trusting one another, practicing forgiveness, and bridging cultures.

People are doing "fairly well" in how they communicate with one another. They are doing "very well" finding common ground and expressing appreciation; doing "well" listening to one another, using technology, and exercising curiosity; and doing "fairly well" engaging conflict.

People are doing "well" in how they treat one another. They are doing "very well" showing kindness; doing "well" practicing humility, feeling compassion, and

Appendix 9

demonstrating love; and doing "fairly well" promoting peace and doing justice.

People are doing "well" in working with one another. They are doing "very well" partnering and working collaboratively; doing "well" discerning and making decisions, being open to change, and being agile organizationally; and doing "fairly well" strategizing and visioning and engaging member's spiritual gifts.

Bibliography

Avon Lake United Church of Christ. "Statement of Welcome." https://avonlakeucc.org/about#StatementofWelcome.
Bass, Diana Butler. *Christianity for the Rest of Us: How the Neighborhood Church Is Transforming the Faith*. San Francisco: HarperCollins, 2006.
Beaumont, Susan. *How to Lead When You Don't Know Where You're Going: Leading in a Liminal Season*. Lanham, MD: Rowman & Littlefield, 2019.
Berscheid, Ellen. "Love in the Fourth Dimension." *Annual Review of Psychology* 61 (2010) 1–25.
———. "Searching for the Meaning of 'Love.'" In *The New Psychology of Love*, edited by Robert J. Sternberg and Karin Weis, 171–83. New Haven: Yale University Press, 2006.
Bobbitt, Linda. "Measuring Congregational Vitality: Phase 2 Development of an Outcome Measurement Tool." *Review of Religious Research* 56.3 (September 2014) 467–84.
Bridges, William. *Managing Transitions: Making the Most of Change*. 3rd ed. Philadelphia: Da Capo, 2009.
Brochard, Paul, and Alissa Newton. *Vital Christian Community: 12 Characteristics of Healthy Congregations*. New York: Church Publishing, 2022.
Brubaker, David. "Three Marks of Healthy Congregations." https://www.congregationalconsulting.org/three-marks-of-healthy-congregations/.
Brueggemann, Walter, ed. *Hope for the World: Mission in a Global Context*. Louisville, KY: Westminster John Knox, 2001.
———. *Truth and Hope: Essays for a Perilous Age*. Edited by Louis Stulman. Louisville, KY: Westminster John Knox, 2020.
"Church Leadership Connection Leadership Competencies." Presbyterian Church (USA). https://www.pcusa.org/site_media/media/uploads/clc/pdfs/leadership_competencies_definitions.pdf.
Cone, James H. *God of the Oppressed*. Rev. ed. Maryknoll, NY: Orbis, 1997.
Ehrich, Tom. *Church Wellness: A Best Practices Guide to Nurturing Healthy Congregations*. New York: Church Publishing, 2008.

Bibliography

Evangelical Lutheran Church of America. "Congregational Vitality: Stories and Learning." https://blogs.elca.org/congregationalvitality/.

Faith Communities Today. "FACTs on Spiritually Vital Congregations: FACT 2020 National Survey of Congregations." https://www.hartfordinternational.edu/sites/default/files/2022-09/FACTs-on-Spiritually-Vital-Congregations-Report_Sep-2022%20%281%29.pdf.

———. "Twenty Years of Congregational Change: The 2020 Faith Communities Today Overview." https://faithcommunitiestoday.org/wp-content/uploads/2021/10/Faith-Communities-Today-2020-Summary-Report.pdf.

Fehr, Beverly. "The Social Psychology of Love." In *The Oxford Handbook of Close Relationships*, edited by Jeffry A. Simpson and Lorne Campbell, 202–3. New York: Oxford University Press, 2013.

Future Earth. "Risks Perceptions Report 2020: 1st Edition." https://futureearth.org/wp-content/uploads/2020/02/RPR_2020_Report.pdf.

Gibb, Jack R. "Defensive Communication." *Journal of Communication* 11.3 (September 1961) 141–48.

"Global Risks Perceptions Report 2021." Future Earth, Sustainability in the Digital Age, and International Science Council. Future Earth Canada Hub, 2021. https://doi.org/10.5281/zenodo.5764288.

Kirkpatrick, Thomas G. *Better Ways to Better Relationships in the Church: Guidelines for Practicing Humility, Experiencing Empathy, Feeling Compassion, Showing Kindness, Expressing Appreciation, and Doing Justice*. Eugene, OR: Wipf & Stock, 2021.

———. *Communication in the Church: A Handbook for Healthier Relationships*. Lanham, MD: Rowman & Littlefield, 2016.

Kittel, Gerhard, ed. *Theological Dictionary of the New Testament*. Vol. II. Grand Rapids: Eerdmans, 1967.

Kwok, Pui-lan. *Postcolonial Imagination and Feminist Theology*. Louisville, KY: Westminster John Knox, 2005.

———. *Postcolonial Politics and Theology: Unraveling Empire for a Global World*. Louisville, KY: Westminster John Knox, 2021.

Lopez, Shane J. *Making Hope Happen: Create the Future You Want for Yourself and Others*. New York: Atria, 2013.

Macy, Joanna, and Chris Johnstone. *Active Hope: How to Face the Mess We're in with Unexpected Resilience and Creative Power*. Rev. ed. Novato, CA: New World Library, 2022.

Magyar-Moe, Jenna L. "Hope Projects to One's Future Self." In *Activities for Teaching Positive Psychology: A Guide for Instructors*, edited by Jeffrey J. Froth and Acacia C. Parks, 137–42. Washington, DC: American Psychological Association, 2013.

Mann, Alice. *The In-Between Church: Navigating Size Transitions in Congregations*. Herndon, VA: Alban Institute, 1998.

Michigan Conference. "Healthy Congregations." https://michiganumc.org/healthy_congregations.

Bibliography

Moltmann, Jurgen. *The Spirit of Hope: Theology for a World in Peril.* Louisville, KY: Westminster John Knox, 2019.

———. *Theology of Hope: On the Ground and the Implications of a Christian Eschatology.* Minneapolis: Fortress, 1993.

Niles, Damayanthi M. A. "A Common Hope Is Always Context-Specific." In *Hope for the World: Mission in a Global Context*, edited by Walter Brueggemann, 107–14. Louisville, KY: Westminster John Knox, 2001.

North/West Lower Michigan Synod. "REVIVE." https://mittensynod.org/docs/REVIVEBrochure.pdf.

Office of the General Assembly. "Church Leadership Connection." https://oga.pcusa.org/section/mid-council-ministries/clc.

———. "Understanding the CLC Competency Survey." https://oga.pcusa.org/section/clc/clc/understanding-clc-competency-survey/.

Pew Research Center. "Religious Landscape Study." https://www.pewresearch.org/religion/religious-landscape-study/.

Pohl, Christine D. *Living into Community: Cultivating Practices That Sustain Us.* Grand Rapids: Eerdmans, 2012.

Presbyterian Church (USA). "Developing the Seven Marks of Vital Congregations." https://www.presbyterianmission.org/wp-content/uploads/VitalCongManualWeb5.7.19.pdf.

———. "Immediate Toolkit for Vital Congregations: Developing the 7 Marks of Congregational Vitality." https://www.fpcsb.net/wp-content/uploads/2019/02/Vital-Congregations-Toolkit.pdf.

———. "Vital Congregations." https://www.presbyterianmission.org/ministries/theology-%20formation-and-evangelism/vital-congregations.

Rand, Kevin L., and Jennifer S. Cheavens. *The Oxford Handbook of Positive Psychology.* 2nd ed. New York: Oxford University Press, 2011.

Rendle, Gilbert R. *Leading Change in the Congregation: Spiritual and Organizational Tools for Leaders.* Herndon, VA: Alban Institute, 1998.

Restorative Church. "Healthy Congregations." https://restorativechurch.org/welcome-to-restorative-church-2/restorative-practices/healthy-congregations.

Rivers, Prince. "Intergenerational Ministry Is Countercultural," June 24, 2024. https://alban.org/2024/06/24/intergenerational-ministry-is-countercultural/.

Rowe, C. Kavin. *Leading Christian Communities.* Grand Rapids: Eerdmans, 2023.

Smith, Donald P. *Congregations Alive: Practical Suggestions for Bringing Your Church to Life Through Partnership in Ministry.* Philadelphia: Westminster, 1981.

Snyder, C. R. *The Psychology of Hope: You Can Get There from Here.* New York: Free, 1994.

Steinke, Peter L. *A Door Set Open: Grounding Change in Mission and Hope.* Lanham, MD: Rowman & Littlefield, 2010.

Bibliography

———. *Healthy Congregations: A Systems Approach*. Herndon, VA: Alban Institute, 1996.

———. *Healthy Congregations: A Systems Approach*. 2nd ed. Herndon, VA: Alban Institute, 2006.

———. *Uproar: Calm Leadership in Anxious Times*. Lanham, MD: Rowman & Littlefield, 2019.

Stewart, John. *Personal Communicating and Racial Equity*. Dubuque, IA: Kendall Hunt, 2016.

Thiessen, Joel, et al. "What Is a Flourishing Congregation? Leader Perceptions, Definitions, and Experiences." *Review of Religious Research* 60.1 (2019) 13–37.

United Church of Christ. "Congregational Vitality and Ministerial Excellence: Intersections and Possibilities for Ministry." https://new.uccfiles.com/pdf/UCC-Congregational-Vitality-and-Ministerial-Excellence-Report.pdf.

United Methodist Church. "Bishops Support Church Reforms, Accountability." https://www.umnews.org/en/news/bishops-support-church-reforms-accountability.

———. "UMC Call to Action." http://s3.amazonaws.com/Website_Properties/connectional-table/documents/call-to-action-congregational-vitality-towers-watson-report-with-appendices.pdf.

———. "The UMC Vital Congregations Planning Guide." http://s3.amazonaws.com/Website_Properties/how-we-serve/documents/vital-congregation-planning-guide.pdf.

Vibrant Faith Projects. "Thriving Congregations Characteristics." https://www.vibrantfaithprojects.org/thriving-congregations-characteristics.html.

Wilkerson, Isabel. *Caste: The Origins of Our Discontents*. New York: Random House, 2020.

Wink, Walter. *The Powers That Be: Theology for a New Millennium*. Minneapolis: Augsburg Fortress, 1998.

Wong, Arch, et al. *Signs of Life: Catholic, Mainline, and Conservative Protestant Congregations in Canada*. Toronto, ON: Tyndale Academic, 2021. https://doi.org/10.1007/s13644-018-0356-3.

World Economic Forum Global Risks. "Global Risks Perception Survey 2022–2023." https://www3.weforum.org/docs/WEF_Global_Risks_Report_2023.pdf.

Wright, Vinita Hampton. "Discernment at Different Stages of Life." https://www.ignatianspirituality.com/discernment-different-stages-life.

www.ingramcontent.com/pod-product-compliance
Lightning Source LLC
Chambersburg PA
CBHW051105160426
43193CB00010B/1316